Galatea

John Lyly

Adapted by Emma Frankland and Subira Joy

Edited by Andy Kesson

methuen | drama

LONDON • NEW YORK • OXFORD • NEW DELHI • SYDNEY

METHUEN DRAMA
Bloomsbury Publishing Plc
50 Bedford Square, London, WC1B 3DP, UK
1385 Broadway, New York, NY 10018, USA
29 Earlsfort Terrace, Dublin 2, Ireland

BLOOMSBURY, METHUEN DRAMA and the Methuen
Drama logo are trademarks of Bloomsbury Publishing Plc

First published in Great Britain 2023

Cover photo by Holly Revell

Title design by Frankie Fagerty

A catalogue record for this book is available from the British Library.

A catalog record for this book is available from the Library of Congress.

ISBN: PB: 978-1-3504-2670-2
ePDF: 978-1-3504-2671-9
eBook: 978-1-3504-2672-6

Series: Modern Plays

Typeset by Mark Heslington Ltd, Scarborough, North Yorkshire

To find out more about our authors and books visit
www.bloomsbury.com and sign up for our newsletters.

Galatea

By John Lyly

Newly adapted by Emma Frankland and Subira Joy

Edited by Andy Kesson

Presented by Marlborough Productions

Co-produced by Emma Frankland, Marlborough Productions, Wildworks and Andy Kesson

Commissioned by Brighton Festival

Supported by Arts Council England, Arts & Humanities Research Council, Attenborough Centre for the Creative Arts, Hall for Cornwall, 101 Creation Space, Jerwood Arts, National Theatre's Generate programme, the Before Shakespeare, Box Office Bears, Diverse Alarums and TIDE research projects, and Worthing Theatres and Museum

Attenborough Centre for the Creative Arts

Arts and Humanities Research Council

worthing theatres and museum

Brighton Festival

Hall for Cornwall
The Generate Programme

National Theatre
WILDWORKS

EMMA FRANKLAND

MARLBOROUGH PRODUCTIONS

JERWOOD ARTS

Supported using public funding by
ARTS COUNCIL
ENGLAND
LOTTERY FUNDED

CAST (in order of appearance)

Sophie Stone	Venus
Femi Tiwo	Galatea
Antonia Kemi Coker	Tityrus/Alchemist
Wet Mess	Cupid
Charlotte Arrowsmith	Telusa
Macy-Jacob Seelochan	Phillida
Ralph Bogard	Melebeus/Journalist
Steve Jacobs	Neptune
Richard Peralta	Rafe
Bea Webster	Hebe
Nadia Nadarajah	Diana
Charmaine Wombwell	Eurota
Ashleigh Wilder	Ramia
Vicky Abbott	Larissa
Caz Teague	Peter

All other roles played by community chorus including: Susan Bishop, Joana Cardoso, Jorge Santos, Scilla Allen, Wenying Wu, Erin Enfys, Ruby Woodhead, Helen McDonald, Beth McDonald, Elaine Woodhead, Eve Whittingham, Jen Lindsey-Clark, Abby Gedge, Sophia Trewick, Teresa O'Connell, Barbara Purves, Caroline Whiteman, Emma Castledine, Claire Ayres, Tim Wild, Clara Sintra-Hall

The Children's Chorus is performed by ThirdSpace Theatre including: Amali Gill, Remy Archdeacon, Bea Twardzik, Ivy Corlett, Rosa Eden-Green, Jowan Frankland, Soli Hougham, Isis O'Farrell, Nina Wilson, Berry Bay Banks, Zoe Card, Kalindi Coe, Tegwen Edwards, Isla Feniuk, Clara Sintra-Hall

COMPANY

Director	Emma Frankland
Director	Mydd Pharo
Associate Director	Duffy
Associate Director	Andy Kesson
Dramaturg	Subira Joy
Costume Design	Mydd Pharo
Set Design	Mydd Pharo
Associate Designer	Ellie WIlliams
Assistant Designer	Ica Niemz
Lighting and Co-Video Design	Joshua Pharo

Co-Video Design and Production Electrician	Sarah Readman
Caption Design	Joshua Pharo, Sarah Readman
Musical Director and Composer	Vicky Abbott
Sound Designer and Sound System Designer	Xana
Sound Design Associate/ Performer	Kayodeine
Additional Shanty Composition	Richard Peralta
Design Maker	Katy Hoste
Design Maker	Bryony Harrison-Pettit
Costume Supervisor	Maria Eva Russo
Wardrobe Assistant	Kit Wright
Costume Makers	Emma Sandham-King, Jess Eaton, Clare Bryant, Jody Dean, Caz Hicks, Caitlin Shaw, Cazz Smith
Main Stage build	Roosters Wood
Team	Rufus Maurice, Gabrielle Osmond, Maurice Chetwyn-Wood, Alan Munden
Additional Design Team credits	Lee Bennett, Simon Bagnall, Luke Wood
BSL Coordinator	Duffy
BSL Performance Interpreter	Sue MacLaine
Our many BSL interpreters	
Choir Coordinator	Aneesa Chaudhry
Volunteer Coordinator	Melanie Kalay
Community Chorus Director and Movement Director	Tanushka Marah
Community Chorus Facilitator	Anthea Clarke
Fight Director	Ella Pennycott
Intimacy Coordinator	Tigger Blaize
Production Manager	Lexi Zelda Stevens
Deputy Production Manager	J'me Howard
Company Stage Manager	Nemo Martin
Assistant Stage Manager	Florian Lim
Production Runner	Elliot Webster-Mockett

Technical Stage Manager	Al Orange
Heads of Lighting and Video	Jodi Rabinowitz and Richard Goodacre
Lighting Technicians	Orion Slater and Eren Celikdemir
Heads of Sound	Hazel Warren-Cooke
Additional Crew	Harry 'Forks' Lane, Andy Smith, Killian Doherty, Matt Royston-Bishop, Victor Hagger, Al Carter, Simon Carter, Tim Hogg
Executive Producer	David Sheppeard
Executive Producer	Emma Hogg
Executive Producer	Lauren Church
Executive Producer	Emma Frankland
Executive Producer	Andy Kesson
Producer	Lee Smith
Assistant Producer	Fee Hudson Francis
Wildworks General Manager	Gwen Scolding
Wildworks Finance Manager	Debra Gristwood
Marlborough Productions General Manager	Amy Greenwood
Diverse Alarums Research Project	Erin Julian, Andy Kesson, S. L. Nelson
Principal Investigator	Andy Kesson
Co-Investigator	S. L. Nelson
Post-Doctoral Researcher	Erin Julian
Marketing Officer	Kamari Romeo
PR	Elin Morgan
Website Design	Zed Gregory
Graphic Design	Frankie Fagerty
Local Engagement Officer	Emma Criddle
Access Manager	Tarik Elmoutawakil
Access Coordinator	Fee Hudson Francis
Wellbeing Practitioner	Josetta Malcolm
Massage Therapist	Ana Bott
Access Consultant	Merry Cross

FOR BRIGHTON FESTIVAL

Andrew Comben	Chief Executive
Beth Burgess	Festival Executive Producer
Polly Barker	Festival Outdoor Producer
Sally Scott	Festival Producer
Dan Lake	Outdoor Production Manager
Carole Britten	Director of Marketing
Hayley Wills	Head of Communications
Emma Gilbert	Acting Head of Marketing
Rosie Blackwell-Sutton	Marketing Manager
Jo Burnham	Senior Marketing Officer
Sarah Wilkinson	Head of Visitor Services
Katie McMurray	Visitor Services Manager
Eleanor Young	Festival Duty Event Manager

Sophie Stone (she/her), Venus

Sophie Stone is Co-Founder of the Deaf & Hearing Ensemble Theatre Company, Associate Artist for The Watermill Theatre & Pentabus Theatre; is on the RADA Committee; and works as a translator and consultant for several TV, film and theatre companies. She has also edited for Arachne Press Poetry.

Theatre includes: *Othello* (The Watermill Theatre); *The Curious Incident Of The Dog In The Night Time* (NT/Frantic Assembly Tour); *The Living Newspaper* (The Royal Court); *The New Tomorrow* (The Young Vic); *The Beauty Parade* (Wales Millennium Centre); *As You Like It* (Shakespeare's Globe); *Emilia* (Shakespeare's Globe/West End); *A Midsummer Night's Dream* (The Watermill Theatre); *Jubilee* (Lyric, Hammersmith/Manchester Royal Exchange); *The Greatest Wealth* (The Old Vic); *The Government Inspector* (Birmingham Rep/UK Tour); *Herons* (Lyric, Hammersmith); *Mother Courage and Her Children* (National Theatre); *Mine* (Shared Experience); *Frozen* (Birmingham Rep); *Two* (Southwark Playhouse); *The Bloody Great Border Ballad Project* (Northern Stage); *In Water I'm Weightless* (National Theatre of Wales); *Pandora* (Arcola); *Woman Of Flowers* (Forest Forge/UK Tour); and *Multiplex*, *Fen* and *You Make Me Happy (When Skies are Grey)* at The Watermill.

Television includes: *The Chelsea Detective* (2), *Moving On*, *Two Doors Down* (2), *Shakespeare & Hathaway*, *Shetland*, *The Crown*, *Doctor Who*, *Mapp and Lucia*, *Moonstone*, *Marchlands*, *Midsomer Murders* (2), *Small World*, *Holby City*, *Casualty* (2) and *FM*.

Film includes: *Name Me Lawand*, *Retreat* (awarded Best Actress Award, Clin d'Oeil Festival), *My Christmas Angel*, *Confessions* and *Coming Home*.

Writing includes: *Listen Harder* essay series (BBC Radio 3), *Beethoven* essay series (BBC Radio 3), *Beethoven Can Hear You* (BBC Radio 3 Drama), *Multiple Scenes of Destruction* (The Bunker Theatre), *Maybe* (Paines Plough/CTWIF), *Butterfly* (Talking Bodies/Hot Coals), *SignHealth* (DV), *Magma Poetry*.

Femi Tiwo (they/them), Galatea

Femi is a queer Nigerian/Togolese multi-disciplinary artist. A Barbican young poet alumni and co-founder of Sistren Collective, their personal work explores ancestral lineages, lost histories and rituals, and what it means to be a first generation Afrobrit raised in Sarf East London. With work spanning across radio, poetry, theatre, film and music, including producing Poetry + Film/Hack with Inua Ellams – there is no art form off-limits when it comes to fully realising the perspective of this emo with a sunshine aura.

Recent credits include: Writing: *Cab Ride* (dir. Femi Tiwo, Ola Jones); *Rights For Whom, Exactly?* (Fly The Flag/Young Vic). Directing: *Sound of the Underground* (Royal Court Theatre); *Cab Ride* (dir. Femi Tiwo, Ola Jones). Performance: *Green Thumb* (Pentabus Theatre); *Losing Joy* (dir. Juliana Kasumu); *Head Over Wheels* (Open Sky); *Little Miss Burden* (Bunker); *Parakeet* (Roundabout); *And The Rest of Me Floats* (Bush Theatre); *Ackee and Saltfish* (BBC3); *Faces* (dir. Joseph Adesunloye); *We Love Moses* (dir. Dionne Edwards); *The Ting* (Channel 4 Random Acts).

Antonia Kemi Coker (she/her), Tityrus

Antonia Kemi Coker is a performer with over 25 years of experience working nationally and internationally in regional and West End theatre, TV film and radio, as well as in Young People's theatre, Forum Theatre, Street Theatre and site-specific theatre. Kemi has worked on numerous projects with Chuck Mike's Collective artists. Her recent work includes a Jack Daniels advert filmed in the Ukraine, work with the theatre company Wake The Beasts' project which deals with health care professionals' experiences during COVID-19. She was a cast member on *I am Kevin* with Wildworks. Kemi has recently finished working on *Beyond Lyrics* at The Tobacco Factory in Bristol with Beyond Face Theatre Company.

Wet Mess (they/them), Cupid

Wet Mess is an artist who works across multiple art forms including visual art, drag, dance, theatre, and choreographing videos for Will Young and London Grammar. Recently they were part of Travis Alabanza's *Sound of the Underground* (Royal Court), which received 5 stars in the *Guardian*, and winner of *Not Another Drag Competition* (RVT, 2021).

Charlotte Arrowsmith (she/her), Telusa

Charlotte studied Theatre, Arts, Education and Deaf Studies at Reading University. She has worked on a variety of projects and with a number of theatre companies such as Facefront, Handprint, Deafinitely Theatre, Half Moon, The Globe and the RSC. Charlotte specialises in children/youth theatre and workshops as an actor, director and workshop leader. She also works as a creative bilingual BSL consultant. Charlotte trail-blazed her way into the mainstream industry with the RSC in 2018 playing Cassandra in *Troilus and Cressida*, and was in their 2019/20 season as Audrey in *As You Like It* and Curtis in *The Taming of the Shrew*. She was the first Deaf BSL actor to work with the RSC as well as understudying a principle role played by a hearing actor. Charlotte became an RSC associate artist as well as associate learning practitioner. Her recent works include *Macbeth* at Leeds Playhouse; the BBC series *This is Going To Hurt*; and a new comedy series soon to be released on Channel 4, *Entitled*.

Macy-Jacob Seelochan (she/they/he), Phillida

Macy-Jacob Seelochan is an actor, writer and music producer from Nottingham. A graduate from Central, MJ's stage credits include *Groove* (Shoreditch Town Hall), *Nevergreen* (Arcola Theatre), *Midsummer Night's Dream* (Nottingham Playhouse) and *Dear Elizabeth* (Gate Theatre). Screen credits include *Shadow & Bone* (Netflix), *Plaggy Bag* (BFI), and two self-produced short films, *Mundane Living* and *A Casting Room*, the latter being a finalist at Pinewood Studio's Lift-Off Festival and available on YouTube. MJ was the 2022 Creative Associate at The Nottingham Playhouse, and as such created their first solo stage show, *Jacob Wants His Grandad*, which previewed at The Pleasance Islington and London Theatre Deli.

Ralph Bogard (he/him), Melebeus

Ralph Bogard has performed on the West End to the Fringe in various plays, musicals and performance projects. Some theatre credits include *A Midsummer Night's Dream* (Shakespeare's Globe), *Nativity! The Musical* (Birmingham Rep), *Bridgerton* (Secret Cinema), *April In Paris* (Hamburg), *Drood!* (Arts Theatre), *The Process* (Bunker Theatre), *Joseph* (UK tour), *RENT* (London), *Ushers: Musical* (Charing Cross Theatre), *Branded* (Old Vic), *Something Something Lazarus* (Kings Head) and *Saucy Jack* (Leicester Square Theatre and Edinburgh). He also has credits in film and TV, plus is the resident host of 'The Prince Charles Cinema' and 'Camp John Waters' (USA), where he interviews Hollywood stars and directors. Find out more @RalphBogard.

Steve Jacobs (he/him), Neptune

Steve Jacobs trained at Guildhall. Credits include *El Senoir Gallindez* at The Gate, *Constant Couple*, *Macbeth* and *The Tempest* at RSC, *School For Scandal* at Haymarket and a tour of Brazil with Dudendance. Steve has worked with many Cornish companies including on *Wolf's Child*, *Souterrain* and *The Passion* with Wildworks, *Very Old Man With Enormous Wings* with Wildworks and Kneehigh, *Waiting For Godot* with Miracle, and *Goodnight Mr Tom* with The Minack Company. He has also worked with English Touring Opera playing King Lear and on NoFit State Circus' *Immortal*. TV and film work includes *Wycliffe*, *Doc Martin*, *The Tape*, and *Poldark*.

Richard P. Peralta (they/he), Rafe

Richard P. Peralta is a Deaf, NB, Filipino-American multidisciplinary artist. Recent performances include *Much Ado About Nothing* (UK tour, Ramps on the Moon, Sheffield Theatres), Ella Hickson's *Wendy and Peter Pan* (Leeds Playhouse), originating the lead role of Riz in local Hove writer Hilmi Jaidin's musical *Cruel, Inhuman, and Degrading*. Other recent works include writing, performing and directing short film *Champorado* (Chocolate Rice) via New Earth Theatre & E.D.E.N. Films, and contributing to Titilola Dawudu and Tamasha Theatre's *Hear Me Now, Volume 2* as a playwright. Richard also works in EDI/social justice, counselling, education, psychology and rugby.

Bea Webster (they/them), Hebe

Bea is a Deaf, queer, neurodiverse, non-binary Scottish-Thai actor, writer, access/BSL/caption consultant and drag artist. Bea graduated with a BA Performance in British Sign Language and English from the Royal Conservatoire of Scotland in 2018. Bea's recent acting credits include: *Medea* (National Theatre of Scotland); *Everyday, Life It Goes On* (Deafinitely Theatre); *Red* (Polka Theatre); *The Winter's Tale* (Royal Shakespeare Company). Bea was nominated for Best Actor at the Stage Debut Awards 2019 for their role in *Mother Courage and Her Children* (Red Ladder/Leeds Playhouse).

Nadia Nadarajah (she/her), Diana

Nadia trained at International Visual Theatre in Paris and Deafinitely Creative Hub under Deafinitely Theatre, London. Acting credits include *Maryland* and *Midnight Movie* (London's Royal Court Theatre). Other productions include: *A Christmas Carol* (Leeds Playhouse and Bristol Old Vic); *As You Like It* and *Hamlet* (Shakespeare's Globe); *Going Through* (Bush Theatre); *Our Town* and *House of Bernarda Alba* (Royal Exchange Manchester); *Grounded* (Deafinitely Theatre at Park Theatre); *A Midsummer Night's* Dream and *Love's Labour's Lost* (Deafinitely Theatre at Shakespeare's Globe); and award-winning 'Can I Start Again Please' with Sue MacLaine Company. TV credits: *Vampire Academy* and *Coffee Morning Club*. Short film credits: *One More Minute* and *Vox Furem*.

Charmaine Wombwell (she/her), Eurota

Charmaine studied Drama at the University of Hull before fronting and writing for original music projects for several years. In 2013 and 2014 she studied at the London International School of Performing Arts (LISPA, now known as arthaus.berlin) and soon after created her dark clown show, *Scarlet Shambles: It Used to be Me*, playing nationally and internationally. Charmaine later studied in Berlin at The Thomas Prattki Centre of Integral Movement and Performance Practice.

Charmaine's other performance credits include: *Burnt Out In Biscuit Land* (Touretteshero/CTN); *Lilies On The Land* (Apollo Theatre national tour); *The Masked Ball* (Southbank Centre/Unlimited Festival); *Going Through* (Bush Theatre); *Not I* (Mouth, performing in BSL, Touretteshero/Battersea Arts Centre and national tour); *Fram and Dunt* (Push Festival, HOME Manchester); *The Listening Room* (Old Red Lion); *Karagula* (Soho Theatre); *Grounded* (Park Theatre/ Deafinitely Theatre).

Voice over credits: Aimee in *Magic Hands* (CBeebies). Directing credits: Raymond Antrobus' *A Language We Both Know How To Sound Out* (Roundhouse). Charmaine is currently writing her next show which will be at the Edinburgh Fringe this year.

Ashleigh Wilder (they/he), Ramia

Ashleigh Wilder is a Black trans masculine actor-poet-thinker from Yorkshire. They delight in speaking about the unspoken, and as a disabled activist channel multiple disciplines into creating art, facilitating workshops, and educating. Acting credits include: *Macbeth* (Leeds Playhouse); *Brassic* (Sky Max); *The Chatterleys* (BBC R4); *The Film We Can't See* (BBC Sounds); and *Left Behind* (Sky Arts).

Caz Teague (they/them), Peter

Creator of the musical project 'Caz Smiling' which blends music, spoken word and illustration to creatively communicate ideas around mental health and queer identity. Caz was the international guest at the Portugal Slam in Lisbon in October 2018 and the poet-in-residence at the Stanza poetry festival in St Andrews, Scotland, in March 2019, continuing to perform their work regularly at poetry and literary events across the UK. From 2017–2022 they also curated London's only regular three-round Slam, Genesis Poetry Slam, and they are an artist-in-residence at the Vauxhall-based queer cabaret night Bar Wotever, with their first poetry collection 'Good Earth' now out with Burning Eye Books, 2019.

Emma Frankland (she/xyr), Director, Co-Writer and Executive Producer

Emma Frankland is an award-winning writer, performer and theatre maker, originally from Cornwall in the UK.

Visually stunning and playfully destructive, her practice contains strong imagery which is often messy, intense and celebratory. Recent work has centred issues of gender and identity (originally published by Oberon Books as *None of Us is Yet a Robot – Five Performances on Gender Identity and the Politics of Transition*).

'Emma Frankland is the punk rock angel of your dreams and nightmares ...' (The Stage)

Emma's diverse collection of work includes: *We Dig* (a show which literally demolished Ovalhouse Theatre with a company of trans women and femmes); an anarchic adaptation of *Don Quijote* which was featured in the British Council Showcase; and *Gender Messy* – a show for young people created with her son, Joey.

She also works as a director and dramaturg and has collaborated with many artists including Rachel Mars, Travis Alabanza and Harry Clayton Wright, and with multiple organisations in the UK and around the world including the Young Vic, Buddies in Bad Times, Stratford International Festival, the BBC and Marlborough Productions. Her work has been performed around the world and she has performed live in Sao Paolo, Rio de Janeiro, Jakarta, Toronto, Belfast, Paris and throughout the UK.

'This is a body of work that is not only about trans identities and gender fluidity but in which these things become catalysts for an expansive exploration of the kind of lives we want to lead and the kind of world we want to live in. This is vital and extraordinary work' (Andy Field, Forest Fringe)

www.emmafrankland.co.uk

Mydd Pharo (he/they), Director, Set and Costume Designer

Mydd Pharo is an award-winning designer, director and visual dramaturg working in theatre, opera, TV, film and live event, creating both intimate and epic scale installations and productions throughout the UK and internationally. His work primarily focuses on immersive and interactive audience experiences and expands both conventional performance spaces and discovered ones.He is Artistic Director of Wildworks, an international site-specific theatre company specialising in large-scale performances in unusual locations.

Mydd studied Theatre Design at Wimbledon School of Art and Fine Art Installation at Falmouth College of Arts. Mydd has exhibited selected works at the V&A Museum London.

He has also designed works for: Kneehigh Theatre, Wildworks, The Globe, The Royal Court, Punchdrunk, 1418NOW, National Theatre, National Theatre Wales, National Theatre Scotland, Battersea Arts Centre, Lyric Hammersmith, Young Vic, Paines Plough, Stratford East, The Eden Project.

Duffy (he/him), Associate Director and BSL Coordinator

Duffy is an Associate Director for this production, having worked with the team in their R+D two years prior. Duffy is an established BSL consultant/translation support in both theatre and the TV/film industry. Duffy worked on several Shakespeare productions such as the RSC's *As You Like It/The Taming of the Shrew/Troilus and Cressida*. Duffy is currently on tour with *ELF & DUFFY: HEIST* – a comedy show featuring mime, BSL and visual vernacular (VV).

Andy Kesson (he/him), Associate Director, Executive Producer and Diverse Alarums Principal Investigator

Andy Kesson is a theatre historian and teacher who works with experimental, fringe and mainstream theatre companies and practitioners, from Emma Frankland to the Royal Shakespeare Company. He has led research projects on the earliest English playhouses (BeforeShakespeare.com), the history of bears in England (BoxOfficeBears.com) and the contemporary performance of early modern plays (GalateaProject.org), and runs the education platform ABitLit.co. He is the author of *John Lyly and Early Modern Authorship*, the editor of essay collections on print popularity and early English theatre, and works across the fields of literature, performance, archaeology, ancient-DNA analysis, animal studies and queer, trans and disability studies.

Subira Joy (they/them), Dramaturg

Subira Joy is a Black, trans, queer spoken-word performer, writer and activist, based in Brighton. Their work weaves together the personal and political, through experiences and imaginations, spoken with rage, softness, and laughter.

Creator of award winning solo spoken-word show, Subira, and co-creator of Joy-Nduku, they have performed in the UK, Finland and Germany, and were poet-in-residence both at ONCA and Trope in March 2019.

Subira regularly hosts their local poetry open mic, runs workshops, created poetry zine *Doesn't It Set your Teeth on Edge* and is the co-editor of *Trans Kink Zine*. Their current show *Kill the Cop Inside Your Head* will be touring in autumn 2023.

www.subirajoy.co.uk

Nemo Martin (they/them), Company Stage Manager

Nemo is a London-based British East Asian writer and theatremaker. In their many lives they stage-manage trans and BESEA shows, write audio dramas like *Trice Forgotten*, plays like *zaazaa* and *[The Cobbled Streets of Geneva],* musicals like *ASIAN PIRATE MUSICAL*. They are a PhD candidate, researching race and gender in *Les Misérables*. nemomartin.com

Joshua Pharo (he/him), Lighting and Co-Video and Caption Designer

Joshua works as a lighting and video designer across theatre, dance, opera, music, film and art installation.

Recent work includes: *Let The Right One In* (Royal Exchange Manchester); *I Am Kevin* (Wildworks); *Corrina, Corrina* (Headlong Theatre).

Upcoming work includes: *Untitled F*ck M*ss S**gon* (Royal Exchange Manchester & Young Vic); *The Odyssey Episode 5* (National Theatre & Public Acts); *Wolf Witch Giant Fairy* (Royal Opera House); *Woman & Machine* (Royal Opera House).

Sarah Readman (they/them), Co-Video and Creative Caption Designer and Production Electrician

As Creative Captioner and Video Designer: *A Dead Body in Taos* (Bristol Old Vic and UK tour); *The Solid Life of Sugar Water* (Orange Tree Theatre & JMK Award); *Endurance* (Jenny Jackson); *Midnight Movie* (Royal Court, with Joshua Pharo); *Future Bodies* (RashDash, with Joshua Pharo).

As Video Designer: *The Crucible, This Beautiful Future* (Yard Theatre).

As Lighting Designer: *The Burnt City* (Punchdrunk, as Lighting Associate); *Belonging* (Tangled Feet); *Let Loose* (Unicorn Theatre and English National Ballet); *Dirt, WOW EVERYTHING IS AMAZING, Fire in the Machine, Phenomena: a Beginner's Guide to Love and Physics* (Sounds Like Chaos); *Voodoo* (Project O); *punkplay* (Southwark Playhouse).

Xana (refer to as name only), Sound Designer and Sound System Designer

Xana is a freestyle live loop musician, composer, spatial sound artist and vibrational sound designer. Xana is also a music science and technology lead at music research label Inventing Waves, where Xana develops accessible sound systems for live art spaces and research sensory audio experiences with scents, touch and raw materials in Xana's music-making process. Xana deconstructs words and found sound in live performances to make improvisational soundscapes, experimental effects and protest music. Xana is also a sound arts and music tech facilitator providing workshops to various youth groups and local community organisations.

Kayodeine (she/her), Sound Designer

Kayodeine is a Black trans femme sound designer and performing electronic musician and DJ working across theatre, film, nightlife, performance art and music with a focus on amplifying marginalised stories and experimentation, constantly referencing her identity, heritage and culture in her work. View her work here: *linktr.ee/kayodeine*

Ellie Williams (she/her), Associate Designer

Ellie is a visual artist and designer working both independently and collaboratively across disciplines. She is an associate artist with Wildworks and has also worked with The Eden Project on large-scale, narrative-led event design and realisation since 2006. For Wildworks, she has spent over 15 years working across the UK and beyond to create designs that bring stories to life, with communities, in unexpected locations and non-traditional performance spaces. Ellie is based in Cornwall where she relocated to study Fine Art at Falmouth College of Arts in 2002. Her practice and interests are rooted in the connections we have to place, land and landscape.

Ica Niemz (they/he), Assistant Designer

Ica Niemz is a designer, puppeteer and performance maker. Their recent design work includes: *Merboy* (Clapham Omnibus Theatre); *Solid Life of Sugar Water* (Jmk Award/Offie award winner, Orange Tree Theatre); *Window of Remembrance* – Trans Week of Visibility/Day of Remembrance (Studio 3 Arts); *Beige* (Vault Festival/Online); *LDN Dares Vogue* (Shakespeare's Globe).

As puppet designer: *I Saw a Monster* (National Maritime Museum); *Gender Messy* (Cambridge Junction); *A Midsummer Night's Dream* (Eastville Park Lido).

Ica was awarded a Weston Jerwood Creative Bursary Fellowship as Assistant Designer with Wildworks 2021–2022. His design work received the Chartered Society of Designers Award 2019.

Vicky Abbott (she/they), Musical Director and Composer

Vicky is a choir director and choral composer based in West Cornwall. In the mid 90s they accidentally formed The Singing Nuns and have worked with choirs ever since. They have been Musical Director on several Wildworks projects and have recently composed for *Re-Voice*, a collaboration with theatre director Agnieszka Blonska, exploring intangible cultural heritage. They direct three choirs and their passion is getting everyone to sing even if they think they cannot!

Maria Eva Russo (she/her), Costume Supervisor

Born and bred in Buenos Aires, Argentina, Maria Eva Russo is a textile artist and researcher with over 25 years of experience in the creative industries working as a wardrobe professional. She studied Film at Buenos Aires University and has a Master's in Sustainable Design from the University of Brighton, where she also worked as a research assistant for an Interreg project. Eva supervised the shows onboard the Cunard Liners and Celebrity Cruises and led their wardrobe teams for nearly a decade. She also taught at the summer workshops of the Central School of Speech and Drama in London for several years, and her textile work has been published in Vogue UK as well as exhibited in Norway and Spain.

Tanushka Marah (she/her), Community Chorus Director and Movement Director

Tanushka Marah is a theatre director, movement director and community facilitator/drama tutor and writer. Her directing work has won several awards and has toured nationally and internationally in Europe and the Middle East. Most recently she was an in-house artist at Brighton Dome with Emma Frankland which is where their collaboration began. She is the artistic director of ThirdSpace Theatre (previously Windmill Young Actors) whose show *Bakkhai* is in Brighton Festival this year. She directed their performance of *Romeo and Juliet* in Hollingdean Skatepark in 2022. She also regularly works with Brighton People's Theatre.

Lexi Zelda Stevens (she/her), Production Manager

Lexi Zelda Stevens is an artist, producer/production manager and career coach who works with artists on ambitious projects. Lexi has been delivering mid- to large-scale music and theatre events for over 14 years. She set up the visual arts programme at Green Man music festival in 2016, where she is Visual Arts Producer, and works on festivals including Glastonbury, Secret Garden Party and Wilderness. She has been Event Manager for Royal Albert Docks Family Weekender and had roles on large-scale events in London's public spaces with Continental Drifts and Team Love. Lexi couldn't afford an MA and has so far been making it up as she goes along, working with organisations including Dance UK and Jerwood Arts. As a coach she works one-to-one with artists and with DWP's Access to Work, UAL and Foundation for Future London's Westfield Eastbank Creative

Futures Fund. She is currently one of nineteen artists awarded a SET Free Studio Prize for a year in Woolwich, London. www.lexizeldastevens.com @helpingartistsmakework

J'me Howard (he/him), Deputy Production Manager

J'me Howard is an entertainment curator and producer/production manager with a background in stage management. He has been delivering theatrical productions, festivals and mid- to large-scale spectacles for over twenty years. He holds a senior role on festivals such as Red Rooster and Secret Garden Party and has worked extensively internationally.

David Sheppeard (he/him), Executive Producer

David co-founded Marlborough Productions in 2009. His work for the company has encompassed a wide range of projects from the ground-breaking national LGBTQIA+ touring theatre project *New Queer of the Block* to the heritage project *Queer* in Brighton. He specialises in live work made for unusual contexts that challenges notions about how and where queer culture can be presented. David is a Clore 18 fellow and previously completed the Arts Fundraising and Philanthropy fellow.

Since 2012 David has been the Co-Artistic Director of The Spire, based at the Grade II listed St Marks Chapel in East Brighton, with ambition of converting this unique space into a creative hub supporting the independent arts community.

As an independent producer David has supported a diverse range of artists to realise their creative visions, most recently Marisa Carnesky and Harry Clayton-Wright.

Emma Hogg (she/her), Executive Producer and Wildworks CEO

Emma was born and grew up in St Austell, Cornwall and after gaining a BA in Human Geography at the University of Lancaster, returned to join the Eden Project where she worked for 13 years with her final role being Eden Live Producer. After nearly 10 years of fleeting moments with Wildworks, she joined the team permanently in December 2014. Emma has been CEO for Wildworks since the death of Founding Director Bill Mitchell in 2017. Recent producing credits include: *Behind the Postcard* – a response from Cornwall for the G7 delegates; *I Am Kevin*; and the soon to be released film version of *I Am Kevin*.

Emma is also a Board Trustee for Theatre Alibi.

Lauren Church (she/her), Executive Producer

Lauren is a creative and strategic arts producer based in Brighton. Her work is focused on diversity, advocacy and sector reform, particularly around issues of disability, mental health, class, race and access. As well as working with Marlborough Productions, Lauren is a freelance professional development consultant for independent artists, one of the producers for Swiss Selection Edinburgh, and is an access support worker for artist and activist, Vijay Patel.

Prior to this, Lauren was senior producer at arts and health charity Something To Aim For where she oversaw the artist development programme working with Le Gateau Chocolat, FK Alexander, Faggamuffins Bloc Party and HighRise Theatre. Lauren also oversaw the implementation of the new accessible digital platform STAF LIVE where she programmed club nights, conversation events and artists digital residencies. She also oversaw national and international partnerships through the festival project The Sick of the Fringe from 2016–2019.

Lauren was previously senior producer at SPILL Festival of Performance 2018, and has worked with a wide array of internationally acclaimed artists including Split Britches, Jodee Mundy Collaborations, Tim Crouch and Bobby Baker.

Lee Smith (they/them), Producer

Lee Smith is the Programme Producer at Marlborough Productions, currently on secondment producing *Galatea*. They have worked with Marlborough Productions since 2018, previously working on their Trans Pride Season and *New Queers on the Block* programme.

As an independent producer, Lee works with live performance and theatre artist Emma Frankland, most recently on *Hearty*, and spoken-word performer and activist Subira Joy, most recently on *Kill the Cop Inside Your Head*. They also work with queer artist-led organisation Milk Presents, most recently on the national tour of *Marty of the Party* and *Trans Filth & Joy* at Manchester Pride.

Diverse Alarums Research Project

Diverse Alarums (GalateaProject.org) is a research project that grew out of Andy Kesson's work on early English theatre (BeforeShakespeare.com) and his collaboration with Emma Frankland on John Lyly's *Galatea*. Perhaps the most frequent stage direction in all early modern drama is 'diverse alarums', which means something like 'Could everyone onstage and backstage please make as much noise as possible?' The disproportionate representation of William Shakespeare in scholarship and performance has aligned early modern drama in the public mind with white, able-bodied, heterosexual, cisgender male narratives, but early modern drama has been calling for diverse alarums all along.

This project challenges this normative trend in 'classical' theatre by mounting a large-scale production of John Lyly's *Galatea*, an early modern play centered around female, trans, queer, disabled and migrant life stories, and featuring almost no adult cisgender men. In doing so, we seek to bring the play to wide-ranging and diverse audiences and experiment with novel ways of foregrounding historical narratives to tell stories that resonate with current socio-political issues. At a time when Shakespeare dominates classical theatre, we seek to permanently reintroduce a forgotten play to the contemporary canon, and thereby challenge the canon's remit in the process.

S. L. Nelson (they/them), Diverse Alarums Co-Investigator

S. L. Nelson is a researcher in the School of Media, Arts and Humanities at the University of Sussex. Operating at the intersection of media and communications, cultural studies and the digital humanities, their work examines the political, economic, social and technological factors involved in contemporary mediation. As the Co-Investigator on the Diverse Alarums project, they are interested in the theoretical, methodological and practical aspects of staging a production of Lyly's *Galatea* that speaks to current socio-political issues around intersectional marginalised identities and the ways in which audiences and communities engage with these issues through the performance.

Erin Julian (she/her), Diverse Alarums Post-Doctoral Researcher

Erin Julian is a Postdoctoral Fellow for the Diverse Alarums project. Her research connects early modern archival records and performance, with particular interest in gender, violence and ethical practice. She is currently writing a new book, *Imperilled Performance*, which explores how musical and dramatic performance led by people of marginalised genders fosters resilience and joy in persecuted royalist and recusant communities in the sixteenth and seventeenth centuries. She is also interested in how performance and song create community in this production of *Galatea*. Her work includes collaborative performance research, including working with Engendering the Stage's laboratory with Stratford Festival in 2018 and co-leading a performance ethnography study around inclusive practice at Stratford. She has published on performance research practice in *Shakespeare Bulletin* and *The Arden Handbook to Shakespeare in Contemporary Performance*.

MARLBOROUGH PRODUCTIONS

Marlborough Productions is a catalyst for queer culture and community.

We are a leading UK producer of queer-led, intersectional performance, parties, heritage and radical community gatherings.

Led by Creative Director Tarik Elmoutawakil and Executive Director David Sheppeard, Marlborough Productions is a pioneering organisation that advances equality and social justice through producing intersectional queer culture.

Over the past ten years, Marlborough Productions has been recognised nationally and internationally for commissioning innovative new work from extraordinary artists, reclaiming spaces to create and share culture and developing communities.

Our Values

- Queer – centring intersectional experiences of identity and how this relates to privilege and/or oppression

- Decolonial – committed to challenging white supremacy and supporting anti-racist action

- Rigorous – realising cultural projects to the best of our ability to ensure enriching experiences.

- Caring – working with artists and communities in an accessible way that prioritises People

- Responsive – welcoming critique and striving to do better

- Joyful – recognising the importance of joy for all LGBTQIA+ people in a world that often tries to rob us of it.

WILDWORKS

Wildworks is the UK's leading landscape theatre company. From our base in Cornwall we make site-specific theatre with communities locally, nationally and internationally. We reach audiences and collaborators all over the globe. Everyone is invited.

Our work attracts people who do not go to the theatre. We're to be found on beaches and woodlands, car parks, nightclubs and disused quarries, anywhere from derelict department stores to medinas, and from refugee camps to castles.

Collaboration and partnerships are central to our process. The lived experience of local people is at the heart of our work and without their participation, the work cannot happen.

Our process starts with a conversation, often with marginalised communities, who help us shape the telling of everyday human stories in ways that are familiar and re-imagined.

We started in Cornwall, and that remains our emotional and physical home. Many of our company members and associates live here and we draw inspiration from Cornwall's extraordinary natural and post-industrial landscape. We continue to build on Cornwall's long history of working outdoors, turning Cornwall's lack of infrastructure into a positive, by working in the landscape rather than traditional theatre venues.

Our practice is shaped by the defining features of Cornwall: a place in which artists naturally collaborate across artforms and with communities; a peninsula somewhere on the edge that looks outwards to the world.

Our work is predominantly site-specific live performance with elements of exhibition, audio/visual, digital media and film. We tell universal stories in ways that are highly visual, making use of diverse media. Our productions resonate and are enjoyed by people across all ages and cultural backgrounds. An important part of our purpose is to support the next generation of landscape theatre makers and artists.

Everything we do is measured against our values: human, brave, fluid and experimental.

Forewords
Andy Kesson

What do you do if your parent is like, 'OMG you are just totally beautiful and it might get you killed by a monster so I'm going to send you off into the woods where the hags go walking'? What do you do if you fall in love but you have no idea what love is and also your whole life is committed to not being in love? What do you do if your child goes missing and also they are Cupid, God of Love, and then you discover they've been causing havoc everywhere they go and now your arch-enemy Diana has imprisoned them and is pulling their wings off? These are just some of the questions that John Lyly's *Galatea* asks, and maybe answers.

In 1583, around the time *Galatea* was written, one Londoner complained that the strange new spaces in London called theatres were 'Venus's palace'. Venus, Cupid or just someone called Love are major characters in all of the surviving earliest plays performed in these theatres, and *Galatea* is the epitome of this early focus on love in performance. As our company have been discovering, *Galatea* is also a play which revels in the joy of representation. 'Thou hast told what I am, in uttering what thyself is', says Telusa: in this play, characters learn possible identities through the thrill of recognising it in others.

In a period when Shakespeare wrote maybe 40 plays mostly named after grumpy men (and wrote no less than seven plays named after various grumpy men all called King Henry for some reason), *Galatea* is a play named after a non-binary, non-grumpy, non-powerful person in a world unusually full of ordinary working people and a surprising number of female gods and supernatural beings.

At a time when Shakespeare was writing a series of romantic comedies that end with heterosexual marriage, *Galatea* shows us a world in which love is an exclusively queer emotion, where consent matters and where gender transition is proposed as a potential outcome for non-binary lovers. *Galatea* is a play consistently in love and at war with binaries: 'neither is there anything but that hath his contraries', Lyly once wrote, writing in this play that life is 'constant in nothing but inconstancy'. Life is always changing, constant and inconstant all at once. Binaries are so deeply embedded into Lyly's play that our company has given Lyly a binary sign name: on the one hand, on the other hand.

Binaries abound and explode and implode across this play. 'What strange contraries breed in my mind?' Telusa asks, voicing the kind of question that both John Lyly and Lyly's audiences might ask as they experience this play. Contraries just keep coming, but again and again we discover that what seemed to be opposites in a binary way of thinking then turn out to be more similar than we thought. 'Are Diana's nymphs become Venus's wantons?' Diana asks. Unfortunately for her, the answer is 'yes'. The binaries have collapsed.

In its staging, this is a play that repeatedly sends characters off in directions that take them somewhere else. 'I follow, I run, I fly,' says Rafe, without really knowing whether it is they go. 'I will, I dare not,' says Phillida about her own exit from the stage. 'Rove then no matter whither,' sings Rafe: go for a wander, wherever you may end up. Cupid is, in part, up to mischief because he has nothing else to do and nowhere else to be. In lieu of a to-do list, 'I will practice a while in these woods', 'whilst I truant from my mother'. This is, after all, a play about people running away from a tree by escaping into the woods, which is not where I would go if I was trying to avoid trees. This is a play in which everyone is in some form of migration, place-seeking, safe spaces to be.

It is a play in which gender slips, again and again, between any muddled attempt to divide it into binaries. Characters wish to undo their own gender ('Would I were no woman,' says Eurota) and can see and articulate the multiple gender possibilities in each other ('He might well have been a woman,' says Phillida of Galatea). Phillida ends Act Four, in the final line before the play tries to find its conclusion, committing to follow Galatea offstage, referring to them with two potential pronouns: 'I will after him, or her'. It is this acknowledgement of, and insistence on, their lover's non-binary identity that premises their love for them.

Galatea is a play written in a real London that casually subjugated women to men. It is set in a fictional patriarchal world which finds safety for its inhabitants only by regularly killing off its least powerful members. But, despite this, it is a play whose characters insist, with glorious regularity, that 'it is pity you are not a woman', that 'it is no second thing to be a woman'.

Contemporary theatre often trains us to think of classical drama as elite, expensive, exclusionary and difficult. In its own time, early modern performance could be for almost anyone. The playhouses were built, owned and run by ordinary working people for ordinary working people. *Galatea* was written for a playhouse owned by a woman, Anne Farrant, performed in front of Queen Elizabeth I, and published by the first woman to publish plays, Joan Brome. It is entirely circumscribed by female agency.

Galatea is an unusual early modern play in many other ways. It is set in England, by the Humber, as we learn from its very first line. This itself is unusual, but then we also discover that this Humber world is full of Roman gods and a village made up of people with Latin names. The play could not lean harder on this binary paradox if it tried: the characters defined as locals in this play – Tityrus, Galatea, even Diana – all have strikingly non-English names, whilst the characters defined as migrants – Rafe, Peter, Dick – all sound like people you might bump into on a sixteenth-century London pub crawl or, indeed, by the Humber.

It would be easy to take the play's reference to the Humber, its setting by this waterway, for granted, but the estuary in fact marks an important historical boundary-marker in England that was of particular interest when Lyly was writing. In a play written just a few years after *Galatea*, *Locrine*, Humber is a character, a Hun who invades Britain. Humber is defeated, forced to wander the land hungry and eventually drowns himself in the body of water which then takes his name. The Humber reminds us of a time before England became a unified country, since it marks an important boundary between medieval kingdoms, a fact that survives in modern English in the regional name Northumbria, which marks out the people living north of the Humber as somehow different from those living south of it. *Galatea* is a play set on a dividing line which asks where Englishness stops and starts, and where its boundaries are. Once again, the play concerns itself with binaries at the point at which those binaries collapse.

Galatea works beautifully as a standalone play, but it is also a sequel *and* a prequel, a kind of *Empire Strikes Back* to the original *Star Wars* and the later *Return of the Jedi*. Lyly's previous play, *Sappho and Phao*, saw the queer Greek poet Sappho turned into a virginal queen who refuses to fall in love with a boy, and avoids an attempt to force her into heterosexuality by stealing Cupid from his mother Venus. Sappho ends her play (with apologies for the plot-spoilers) by promising to 'keep love a toy for ladies', and going further in saying that 'I will keep it only for ladies'. And then we get *Galatea* in which love is indeed a queer toy that no longer troubles cis men. This is a kind of thematic, queer continuity between the two plays, and it is underlined by a narrative continuity in which Cupid plays 'truant from my mother' in the wake of Sappho's intervention, a fact underlined by Venus herself where she is finally reunited with her son: 'How now, sir boy? First with Sappho, now with Diana?' In the third play of the trilogy, *Love's Metamorphosis*, Cupid has grown up into a very different deity, but the audience are once again asked to think about the newer play in terms of *Galatea*. Even as he glories in self-righteousness in *Love's Metamorphosis*, Cupid is asked why he tormented Diana's nymphs in *Galatea*. Across these plays Lyly offers us the London theatre scene's very first trilogy, one which challenges the conventions of heterosexuality and triumphs in the queerer world of Sappho, Galatea and Phillida.

Whilst *Galatea* operates in this long plot extended across two other plays, it also does something new with the idea of multiple plots across one single play. *Galatea* isn't the first English play with multiple plots (which, as we've just seen, include the ones emerging out of *Sappho* and into *Love's Metamorphosis*). But it is the first play written for a London playhouse in which multiple plots are extended across the entire life of the play, from start to finish. This makes it the first such play to ask what happens when you tell a number of stories at the same time, and how on earth you then bring them together into resolution.

Anyone who's seen the film *Crazy Stupid Love* (2011) will be familiar with a story structure which seems to offer two separate plots, then surprises the viewer at the end by suddenly bringing them together. *Galatea* does exactly the same thing, joying in the sudden delight of eliding things which seemed to be defined by being kept apart. Just at the level of human bodies onstage, the play's structure moves us through a succession of scenes featuring one, two, three characters, sometimes very occasionally more than this.

And then a final scene brings everyone together. Neptune comments on this as soon as it starts to happen, when he goes from being alone onstage to suddenly having to share the final scene with two new people: 'I muse not a little to see you two in this place, at this time, and about this matter'. And the final entrance in this final scene also triggers a commentary on these unexpected entrances. Diana is the person in this play who lives in the biggest community, but even she is surprised by all these new final people: 'What are these that so malapertly thrust themselves into our companies?' she asks. This is a question which is about the social mixing of gods, nymphs, parents, children, lovers and migrants, but it's also a question about the stage itself, about dramaturgy: woah, what are all these plots doing converging, as Neptune says, 'in this place, at this time, and about this matter'?

'Malapertly' is a very unusual word, implying disrespect or inappropriateness: Diana cannot believe that all these people are here. The word 'thrust', implying sudden, unexpected, unwanted movement, is a less unusual word conveying a similar idea, and it gives us a flavour of how remarkable Lyly was finding their play even as they wrote it. Something new is happening here.

This is a very different world and stage image compared to Lyly's previous play, Galatea's prequel, Sappho and Phao, which ends with a boy alone in an unfriendly world. This new Galatea world may be malapert, but it is radically and newly full of love.

There have been times when we thought we would never get this production onstage. But 'What is to love, or the goddess of love, unpossible?' What a joy it is to write an introduction to this play alongside some of the fabulous theatremakers who have made sure this production was not unpossible.

Lyly may also have struggled to stage this play: there is evidence that Lyly was writing it in 1583, trying to stage it in 1584, trying to protect it from publication in 1585, staging it (perhaps for the first time, perhaps in revival) in 1588, and publishing it in 1592. This protracted history gives us a window onto the possible reception of the play's queerness in its own time, and makes me feel a bit better about the many years it has taken us to stage our version!

In a dazzling series of images invoked across his various plays, John Lyly thought of performance as magical, physical, supernatural, perhaps a little scary. For example, Lyly calls performance 'the dancing of Agrippa his shadows'; that is, the boogying of a necromancer's demons. Performance is 'a dance of a fairy in a circle', a 'labyrinth of conceits', leaving you, the audience, in the 'doubts wherewith we leave you entangled'. Performance can one minute have 'fluttered by twilight, seeming a swan', but then 'be proved a bat set against the sun', shifting from gorgeous to scary as the light shifts.

Above all, performance changes with its audience, 'resembling water, which is always of the same colour into what it runneth'. Performance, in this model, doesn't actually exist or have definition until the audience sees and processes it, which perhaps explains why Lyly's most common word to describe their plays is 'whatsoever': this-thing-I-cannot-name. In staging this 'Whatsoever we present', the playwright and the production company simply do not know what they are showing, because it is up to the audience. As I write this introductory note, I have no idea what our audience will make of our show. I can't wait to find out!

Duffy

I have two roles within the production of *Galatea*: associate director and BSL consultant. At the start of the process the original text was translated into modern English by Andy Kesson. As BSL consultant I then have the material to play with to translate the text into BSL that is comprehendible to the cast and audience.

The actors using BSL will prepare their own translations before rehearsals; this means that when we meet in the rehearsal space I can guide them and offer alternatives/suggestions. For example, different signs, specific handshapes, rhythms/pace, in keeping with the Lyly style of – *this and that.* I felt it was important to keep the Lyly essence in sign language as much as possible so the deaf audience can have access to this style of theatre.

Not only are we using British Sign Language, but we are also incorporating American Sign Language as well as ad-libbing in various signed languages. We have enjoyed the privilege of borrowing signs from Germany; for example, the sign-name Diana comes from the German for 'god/goddess'. The sign signifies Diana's crown and has become iconic throughout the play.

In the world of *Galatea* the Gods understand each other in both spoken English and BSL/signed languages. Neptune can communicate with Diana and Venus even though they are BSL speakers. And both Venus and Diana can understand Neptune when he speaks. Although disability still exists in the world of *Galatea*, for the Gods barriers to communication do not exist as they are supreme beings.

Transgender identity is a theme that runs throughout the play; however, in British Sign Language we do not use pronouns – you simply point your finger (this is not considered offensive in deaf culture) to make a reference to someone. To determine possessiveness you clench your fist and sign towards the intended person. In other cases you simply address the person with their name and/or sign-name.

As an associate director my responsibility is to ensure that the actors using sign language are understood by a mainstream audience. It is also to make sure that a deaf audience have access to the language of Lyly and can understand the concepts.

Emma Frankland

This production has been coming for 8 years.
Or 15 years.
Or 450 years, depending on where you count from.

There is no doubt in my mind that John Lyly was some flavour of trans person and that *Galatea* is an important piece of trans archival history. This play has lent itself to our production so beautifully – wherever we have adapted and changed the text it has felt as though we were writing in collaboration with Lyly. Nothing felt forced.

I think one of the beautiful things about the play is that it is possible to interpret the identities of the lovers in so many ways – are they two women in love? Are they cis women or trans women? Or both? Or neither?

The only thing that is certain is that Lyly did not write a heteronormative love story. Even the play's offer of a magical gender transition at the end does not mean it is surrendering to cisnormative standards (as has been suggested by some scholars). We don't need to look beyond the current UK media climate to see that a person who changes from one gender to another is not afforded respect. Or that a gender transition (whether due to divine intervention or self meds) does not mean a person becomes, or wishes to become, cis!

I hope that people who do not often see their identities celebrated in classical performance recognise themselves in our telling of the story – it is particularly exciting for me to see a trans-feminine character on stage (in Phillida). We trans girls seldom get seen at all, let alone as lovers – let alone as lovers with happy endings! *Galatea* is truly a radical, trans play.

I first met Andy Kesson as part of the Globe Theatre's 'Read Not Dead' series, where we were part of the mammoth effort to give full rehearsed readings to the plays of all of Shakespeare's contemporaries. We met on *Galatea* – I was playing one of the boys (it was a different life) and, because some things never change, Andy was writing a brilliant introduction.

A number of years later, we were kicking around the idea of a collaboration – the impulse (which I maintain was Andy's) was to approach one of Lyly's plays, but not from the mainstream Western classical theatre tradition – instead to lean into my practice as a queer, trans theatre artist (basically: less words, more fire). *Galatea* seemed the obvious choice – a clearly Very Queer play that seemed never to have had a just revival.

I was intrigued, but only if we could take up the kind of space I felt this play deserved, and so invited the brilliant Mydd Pharo of Wildworks to join the conversation – the idea being that an outdoor production could give us access to scale and an audience who would feel comfortable in seeing a spectacle, rather than treating it as a curiosity.

Our first R&D period in 2016 was supported by Jerwood Foundation and took place in London in their studios. We spent a week with an amazing group of creatives, largely queer and trans, with their own artistic practices and backgrounds and we asked the question – does this play still feel relevant today? The answer was a firm yes.

Our next exploration was a smaller group, who met at Roehampton University. A mix of trans identities – specifically exploring the different gender possibilities of the lovers. We then spent two weeks in Cornwall in 2018 with the intention of taking the play outdoors – this residential saw Hebe sacrificed on a beach and Gods walking across the clifftops, as well as an undeniably magical moment between Steve Jacobs as Neptune, a conch shell and a family of snails.

In 2019, an invitation to Stratford Festival, Ontario provided another two-week intensive study of the play . . . this time working with a group of two-spirit and trans people from Turtle Island as well as myself, Subira Joy and the full cast of the musical, *Billy Elliot*!

The invitation was to run a lab under the title 'Exploring the Trans Canon' – an attempt to define what a trans classical body of work might be. Of course, as we discovered, there is no such thing as a 'trans canon' – largely due to centuries of trans erasure, violence and forgetting. But the work we made in that room proved vital to the way we have worked since, creating a room agreement and centring care as the highest priority in the project, to enable everyone in the room to engage and thrive.

'When you hire people to be themselves, bring their own lived experiences, and represent their communities, additional care is required.'

Post-Stratford, we had a renewed sense of the potential of the show and, during the strange suspension of time caused by 2020 lockdowns, began to make plans with Marlborough Productions to bring our production to Brighton Festival.

There followed a final period of exploration on the text that took place at 101 Creation Space, specifically exploring the use of BSL and centering the amazing Deaf creatives we had been working with from the start. This period also introduced us to many of our final performance company, including our brilliant associate director and BSL co-ordinator, Duffy.

Last year we had our final R&D at the National Theatre Studio, focussing on the characters of Rafe and Peter. Subira and I knew we loved these characters, but not their stories as written by Lyly. So perhaps the boldest aspect of our adaptation was creating new threads for them both – a story, shaped in collaboration with Ammar Haj Ahmad, which creates, for the character of Rafe, a more contemporary migrant experience and, for Peter, an amplification of their role – they become another trans voice in the play. Speaking up, speaking out and ultimately speaking back to the powerful Gods when they overstep!

Now, partway through rehearsals, I am loving seeing the play continue to grow, twist, surprise us and continue to delight the room. I cannot wait to share it with our audiences and with you!

And it doesn't end here. I hope that the text is reimagined by many more people in the future and that we see as many iterations as we see of the plays that *Galatea* inspired – *As You Like it, A Midsummer Night's Dream* . . .

Here is our offer to you . . . take it, change it. It is yours and stories (like Peter says of 'trans magic') cannot be pinned down!

Subira Joy

Who'd have the audacity to rewrite a 450-year-old play? That's a feeling I thought would come up more frequently, but something that we've often said is that it feels like we're working in collaboration with John Lyly, rather than doing a cover version. There's no way we could do this without being so deeply taken in by the way Lyly writes. I found myself being absorbed by the word play, patterns, rhythms and imagery, and the more that I looked at the text, the more I found myself thinking and speaking in the same cadence. Lyly loves a binary – setting up and collapsing binary after binary. Lyly uses binaries to show us characters that are stuck in their ways, trapped in traditions, and unable to see a way out, and that stepping outside of binary thinking allows us to imagine other possibilities and move the story forward. Which I, as a trans non-binary performer and activist, deeply appreciate.

I first got involved in *Galatea* in 2019 when I went with Emma to Stratford Festival, Ontario to do a workshop exploring the idea of a 'trans canon', with a group of two-spirit and trans artists and a group of actors from the festival, where we played with scenes and themes of the play. The ethos that we moved with back then has stayed with us throughout – of prioritising care, centering marginalised narratives, and of inviting people's lived identities to shape the work rather than solely letting the work shape us.

We've approached this process with an attitude of flexibility and openness to new discoveries. Nothing about these words are so precious that they cannot be changed! At the same time, there were things that felt so radical in Lyly's script that we didn't want to touch the language much, but instead dedicate time and energy to ensure Lyly's words would still land and be understood (trans people fall in love and are cute and flirty! A patriarchal God relinquishes his power! Queer joy and gender play!). In that way, much of the rewriting has been a real work of collaboration with the performers. Often, I would have the desire to rewrite something just based on how I was struggling with it on the page, but as soon as the language was in the hands of the performers, it was brilliant!

Some of it did need a big shake up; we've grappled with the racial politics, which felt like our largest conflict with Lyly's politics within the play – how to reflect our decolonial values without sanitising history. There have been moments where we've let ourselves be really bold; bringing in contemporary language and frameworks, writing in entire new scenes, conflating two different characters into one. These changes felt completely audacious, but the permission to change has been intrinsic in what the play is all about! The conclusion of the play is just that; change is vital, and there is only so much we can resist it.

MYDD PHARO
WILDWORKS – Artistic Director
GALATEA – Co-Director, Set and Costume Designer

I was given an opportunity here, a 400-word count to write something …

Instead, I'd like you to use the space below to write, draw or visualise something yourself.

Maybe something about your own story. I hope it's a story of love, honesty, friendship, true equality and one where you face up to the monster that stands in your way.

Don't give in to the continuous challenges, discrimination, the policing of your ideas, the dismissing of who you are, what you know and what you believe in.

Be yourself and always take the WILD path.

Mydd x

Thank you

Worthing Theatres
Callan Davies

Jon Opie
Krishna Istha

All of the amazing creatives who have been on the journey of adapting this play over the past 8 years including:

Selina Thompson
Emily Joh Miller
Alexandrina Hemsley
Kim Tatum
Angela Clerkin
Ash Palmisciano
Kyla Goody
Dylan Frankland
Kellan Frankland
John Frankland
Griffyn Gilligan
Chiron Stamp

Hermi Berhane
Jamal Ajala
Becky Allen
Cole Alvis
Samson Bonkeabantu Brown
Cassandra James
Beric Manywounds
Rhiannon Collett
Scottee
Mary Woodvine
Ammar Haj Ahmad
Mary Malone

Our many BSL interpreters

Jorge and Jo
My Genderation
Rosie Powell
Holly Revell
James Wallace
Harry Clayton-Wright
Stewart Pringle
Ted Witzel
Akila Richards
Caz and the team at SOLD
All at EMAUS
Academic collaboration and support
Arts and Humanities Research Council
The Diverse Alarums advisory board: B. K. Adams, Simone Chess, Nandini Das, Callan Davies, Ben Fowler, Kit Heyam, Sawyer Kempt, Catherine

Richardson, Kirsty Sedgman and John Walker
Pascale Aebischer
Shakespeare Bulletin
Box Office Bears: Archaeology, Archives, Performance
Clare McManus
Jane Kingsley-Smith
Laura Peters
Richard Keogh
Melinda Gough
Natasha Korda
Akila Richards
Sarah from Drift
Luke Skilbeck
Kim Solga
Cathy Waller
Faith Dodkins and the Spire Arts
3rd Shoreham Sea Scouts
Whimsy Teas
Simply Veg

Cloak and Dagger Brewery
Paul Barrow
Okoru
Festival Marquees
Stage Sound Services

White Light
SMART Power – Sebby and Tim
AAA Security
Okuro and Ed Metals

Marlborough Productions would like to thank:

Our board of trustees
Arts Council England
Paul Hamlyn Foundation
Esmée Fairbairn Foundation

Galatea

Characters

The Gods

Neptune *(he/him) is supposed to be in charge. The powerful God of the Sea is disguised as the local MP/mayor of Little Shoreham. He begins the show happily in charge in a world of his own construction.*

Venus *(she/her), Goddess of Love and Beauty – Cupid's mother. 'Love knot' vendor. She is observing for much of the play (distracted by the love of Galatea and Phillida) She arrives at the end and puts the world to rights.*

Cupid *(he/they), adolescent toxic 'little god'. Easily offended, fragile ego, they cause havoc by non-consensually causing Diana's nymphs to be overcome with fierce love and desire.*

Diana *(she/her), Goddess of Chastity and the Moon. Fiercely loyal to her woods and the nymphs in her protection. She will fight for her values and her beliefs. She does not suffer fools gladly and is opposed to Neptune's tradition of sacrifice.*

The Lovers

Galatea *(she/they), a young Black trans person whose understanding of their gender identity unfolds as they fall in love with Phillida. Reluctantly sent into the woods for their own safety by their parent, Tityrus.*

Phillida *(she/her), a young trans girl, living as herself in the community of Little Shoreham. Also sent by her father into the woods in disguise. She falls in love with Galatea and is able to explore her own fluid gender identity as a result.*

The Mortals

Tityrus *(she/her), Galatea's parent. Tityrus is a Black local business owner. She is making a life in this town for herself and her child. She is also the* **Alchemist** *– connected to ancestral knowledge, the alchemy of cooking, of medicine and of magic. She is not always a good employer.*

Melebeus *(he/him), Phillida's dad. Melebeus is a local celebrity and loyal citizen, so his betrayal of Neptune (sending Phillida away in disguise) is a big deal. He is also the* **Journalist** *– a tabloid journalist/broadcaster who attempts to profit from Rafe.*

Hebe *(she/her, later they/them) holds status in the town as a supporter of the Neptune regime. They are also the volunteer immigration enforcement patrol officer. These roles mask their true, queer identity which is only revealed when they become the sacrifice for the Agar and death seems inevitable.*

Rafe *(he/they) is from another place. He is shipwrecked and far from home, family, language and friends. He is attempting to find work in order to survive, but the world he finds himself in is hostile. Rafe sees the audience for who they are.*

Peter *(he/they) is a Black trans person who has been working for the Alchemist for some time. He knows Galatea and can support their trans coming out. He is attempting to steal the Alchemist's tools/ knowledge for concocting trans-affirming potions in order to bring them into community knowledge, but is distracted when he meets the amorous nymphs!*

The Nymphs

Diana's *wards – people who have fled persecution or sought out her protection. They live in the woods and they protest the misogyny and violence of* **Neptune**'s *society.*

Telusa *(she/her) is Diana's second. Committed and smart, strong and direct, impulsive. The contrast when she is overtaken by Cupid is huge. Her name means 'roots'.*

Eurota *(she/her), another in Diana's care, is more of a dreamer than a fighter. Secretive and crafty. But she is loyal to Diana and tries her best to fit in with the goddess's ideals. Her name means 'river'.*

Ramia *(they/them), impulsive and a newer member of Diana's company. Their name means 'branches'.*

Larissa *(she/her), the leader of Diana's chorus, is strong minded and practical, keeping the rest of the nymphs in check. Her name means 'citadel'.*

A note on future casting of this adaptation

This adaptation is mostly faithful to John Lyly's original text, as transcribed by Callan Davies from the 1592 first edition with song lyrics taken from the 1632 edition of six Lyly plays.

It was adapted by Emma Frankland and Subira Joy and edited by Andy Kesson, with BSL support by Duffy. Additional contributions were made by the company and by Nemo Martin and Krishna Istha.

Where lines have been changed or scenes and characters have shifted, this has happened to better reflect the lived identities of the performers playing them as well as the times we are living through.

Whilst there has been no pressure or requirement for the company to bring their individual lived experiences into the rehearsal room, we wanted the play to shift itself to accommodate our company – rather than the other way round. Therefore, in re-performing this play, we encourage you to do the same, making changes to accommodate the needs of your company.

This said, if you are re-performing our adaptation:

– where the script names a character as trans, they must be played by a trans actor;

– where the script names a character as Black, they must be played by a Black actor.

A note on reading the text

We have put stage directions in *italics*.

Stage directions will refer to a character's pronouns as listed at the start of this script. (NB: this may differ from how other characters in that scene may refer to that person.)

Whether a character speaks in Spoken English [ENG], British Sign Language [BSL] or American Sign Language [ASL] will be indicated at the start of the scene.

In our production, Diana, Venus, Hebe, Rafe and Telusa were played by Deaf actors.

The roles of Melebeus, Ramia and Eurota were played by hearing actors who spoke both English and BSL.

The roles of Neptune, Galatea, Phillida, Cupid, Peter and Tityrus were played by hearing actors who spoke no BSL.

All spoken text (BSL or ENG) was creatively captioned throughout and there was a BSL interpreter onstage each night.

Pre-show

As the audience arrive:

The route into the site takes the audience past several scenes which introduce them to the world and themes of the show. In small groups, they are led to the site by a local/dog walker/village official. These scenes might be:

People pulling life jackets from the river which are piling up on the bank.

There is a pop-up encampment which looks like a protest site.

Neptune *and his entourage are having fancy tea and sandwiches on a lawn.*

The 'Neptune Day' County Fair:

As the audience arrive into the main performance area there are different sideshows to see and food and drinks to purchase.

People wear cardboard crowns and carry little tridents on sticks.

An **Alchemist** *attempts to turn base metals to gold. Her child and worker assist.*

People are encouraged to leave their love knots on a fence – tied with ribbons and padlocks to commemorate love.

There are various village fete activities.

There is an exhibition of local children's art showing their ideas of the monster Agar – perhaps one wins a prize?!

The local TV **Journalist** *is recording vox pops and getting the crowd hyped and ready – his daughter and* **Hebe** *assist.*

Shoreham is a nice town. Sussex is a nice county. And when the fair comes around – once every five years – there is a light and cheerful atmosphere. The local schools put on productions of the history of the fair and the vendors tout their wares.

The site of the ancient oak tree is decorated in the centre of the green and dancers gambol around it, while vegetables are judged, fortunes told and old rivalries play out.

In a tent – next to the wonky vegetables – people of all ages are placed on stools and assessed. The search to find 'the beautifullest and most chastest maiden in all the county' is on and debate around the meaning of these words abounds.

And on the edges . . . the edges of the woods. Along the banks of the river . . . eyes are watching.

As ever, there are disagreements and protests – there are those who disagree with the local traditions, make themselves known by stealth: 'No Sacrifice' anonymously daubed on a wall, 'End This Barbaric Tradition' printed on stickers dotted here and there.

And a group, led by people of all ages, come from their encampment in the woods. They stand aside, chanting and holding signs . . . some of the townsfolk ignore them. Some attempt to argue with them – mostly people try and focus on the festivities . . . Drown them out with the music. Keep the traditions alive. Keep the community safe.

Resist change.

And the Gods are always present . . . in their disguises. Always observing – **Neptune**, **Venus**, **Diana**, **Cupid**.

The show starts . . .

Prologue

The love knot trader steps forward and gives the prologue – she is the goddess **Venus**, *in a mortal disguise!* [**Venus** *speaks in BSL.*]

Venus

Hello, audience . . . I'm Venus. Welcome to Little Shoreham!

Like all towns, it is many places at once. There are many stories here.
For some, it smells like violets – for others, it smells like myhrr. The smell of death. I was born in one town, I'll be buried in another – that's the way these things go. We do not stay in one place – the borders between these worlds are thin – and, like life, none of you will experience this story the same way.

Don't mind what the weather's doing – this is England isn't it?! Because your attention and favour is all the sunshine we need.
We start by celebrating the first – your attention. The gift of you being here, with us, today. And we will end with the other – your favour – when you applaud at the end!

If you applaud us. After you've seen what is to come.
Who knows, perhaps when you go home it will be to a different town than the one you left?

And what is to come?
It's a love story. That's why you're here right?!
This is a love story – a story about the absence of love.
Which is a curse.
Let me ask you – how much love are you holding for other people right now? Oh, I don't mean your children, your nan, your lovers . . . although I'm sure you have some of those . . .

She speaks to one person in the audience.

I know *you* do!
How much love are you holding for those you have yet to meet?

Who come from elsewhere?
Who seem different?

The question hangs in the air . . . **Venus** *is waiting. She shrugs.*

Oh look, here come the children! They'll tell you about
the monster . . .

The Children's Neptune Day Celebration:

*As is traditional, the local school puts on a mime show – depicting
the sacrifice of maidens to the monster Agar that keeps the community
thriving.*

Hebe *is bustling them along, prim and proper – they look like they
would be a horrible teacher to have.*

*People are laughing, enjoying the cuteness of it all [it's like the
children's 'Snow White' performance in the film* Parenthood.]

There's a dance and a papier-mâché monster.

Suddenly there is screaming.

The show is disrupted.

A person is screaming, seeming to have lost her mind.

'My daughter! My daughter! They took her . . . No more!
No more!'

*The children are crying and shocked, some watchers try to help, most
look away. The distraught mother is escorted from view.* **Neptune**
*(in his guise as town official) makes some attempt at a joke and
people continue about their business.*

In the midst of this, **Tityrus** *and her child,* **Galatea,** *climb up onto
the stage and begin to speak . . .*

Act One

Scene One

Tityrus (*the Alchemist*) *and* **Galatea**. [**Tityrus** *and* **Galatea** *speak ENG.*]

Tityrus
> The sun doth beat upon us, wherefore let us sit down,
> Galatea and enjoy the fresh air, which softly breathes from
> Adur floods.

Galatea
> And whilst we sit, Mother, you shall recount to me, if it
> please you, for what cause this place was dedicated unto
> Neptune and, er, why you have thus disguised me?

Tityrus
> I do agree, and when thy state and my care be considered,
> thou shalt know this question was not asked in vain.

Galatea
> I willingly attend.

Tityrus
> In times past, where thou seest a heap of small pebbles,
> stood a stately temple of white marble, which was
> dedicated to the God of the Sea (which was quite right –
> being so near the sea).
>
> Here came all such – either venturing by long travel to see
> new countries, or by great traffic to sell merchandise.
>
> But Fortune, constant in nothing but inconstancy, did
> change her copy, as the people their custom, for the land
> became oppressed by supremacist ideology.
>
> The people instead of sharing, became selfish;
> Instead of being inclusive, became insular;
> Instead of having faith, caused friction;
> And they made a prey of that in which they should have

made their prayers, tearing down the temple even with the earth.

This act of vandalism enraged so the god who binds the winds in the hollows of the earth, that he caused the seas to break their bounds, since men had broke their vows, and to swell as far above their reach, as men had swerved beyond their reason.

Then might you see ships sail where sheep feed,
Anchors cast where ploughs go,
Fishers throw their nets, where farmers sow their corn.
Then might you gather froth where now is dew,
Rotten weeds for sweet roses,
And take view of monstrous mermaids, instead of beautiful young maids.

Galatea

To hear these sweet marvels, I would mine eyes were turned also into ears.

Tityrus

But in the end, our country-men repented, and not too late, because Neptune, upon condition, consented to ease their miseries.

Galatea

What condition will not miserable men accept?

Tityrus

The condition was that at every five years' day, the most beautiful and chaste maiden in all the country should be brought unto this place, and here be bound, left for a peace offering unto Neptune.

Galatea

Dear is the peace that is bought with guiltless blood.

Tityrus

I am not able to say that, but he sendeth a monster called the Agar, against whose coming the waters roar, the fowls fly away, and the cattle in the field for terror, shun the banks.

Galatea

And she bound to endure that horror?

Tityrus

And she bound to endure that horror.

Galatea

Doth this monster devour her?

Tityrus

Whether she be devoured of him, or conveyed to
Neptune, or drowned between both, it is not permitted to
know, and it's dangerous to conjecture; now, Galatea, here
endeth my tale, and beginneth thy tragedy.

Galatea

Alas, and why so?

Tityrus

I would thou hadst been less beautiful, or more fortunate,
for thy beauty will make thee to be thought worthy of this
sacrifice.

Despite these curses, the people's customs did not change;
still we shun strangers from our shores, ill-treat the
impoverished and make judgements of persons as if we
had the authority of the gods.

Therefore (to avoid destiny) I think it better to use an
unlawful means than to suffer intolerable grief.

Now hast thou heard the custom of this country, the cause
why this place was dedicated unto Neptune, and the
vexing care of thy fearful parent.

Galatea

Mother, I have been attentive to hear, and by your
patience am ready to answer. Destiny may be deferred,
not prevented; and therefore it were better to offer myself
in triumph, than to be drawn to it with dishonour.

Hath nature (as you say) made me so desired above all,
then shall not virtue make me as famous as others? Do you

not know (or doth over-carefulness make you forget) that an honourable death is to be preferred before an infamous life. I am but a child, and have not lived long, and yet not so childish, as I desire to live forever?!

Virtues I mean to carry to my grave, not grey hairs.

I would I were as sure that destiny would light on me, as I am resolved it could not fear me.

Nature hath given me beauty, virtue courage,
Nature must yield me death, virtue honour.

Suffer me therefore to die for which I was born, or let me curse that I was born, since I may not die for it.

Tityrus
Galatea, to consider the causes of change, thou art too young, and that I should find them out for thee, too, too fortunate.

How do you speak of virtue and honour and have barely lived enough to know what these words mean? These words mean something different for us. Did I not raise you for better? Do I need to remind you that, for us, virtue, honour and destiny are not the same as it is for them?

Your life is not something that you allow to slip through your fingers, your life matters. You carry your ancestors' stories in your bones, how dare you take that for granted? No. You don't get to throw away your precious life. It is your duty to live it.

Galatea
You tell me to live my life, but would it not be the life of another, following the path of another, in the attire of another.

Tityrus
To gain love, the very gods have taken shapes of beasts, and to save your own life art thou too coy to take the attire of a man?

Galatea

They were beastly gods, that lust could make them seem as beasts!

Tityrus

With age it is easy to counsel the young, but it is hard for a child to follow wholesome counsel. You have heard my words, this matter is done, for now.

Exeunt.

Scene Two

Cupid *and* **Telusa**. **Telusa** *has left* **Diana***'s camp and the safety of the protest group – she is fly posting some anti-sacrifice posters, but trying to pass as a regular townsperson.*

Cupid *sees right through her. Perhaps they shoot an arrow into the ground beside her to gain her attention?* [**Telusa** *is Deaf and speaks her lines in BSL –* **Cupid** *can understand and uses BSL or ENG as fits the actor.*]

Cupid

Hey! Most honourable, chaste nymph, are you strayed from your company by chance, or love you to wander solitarily on purpose?

Telusa

Sweet boy, or god, or whatever you be, I would you knew these woods are to me so well known, that I cannot stray though I would, and my mind so free, that to be melancholy I have no cause.

There is none of Diana's train that any can train, either out of their way, or out of their wits.

Cupid

What is that Diana? A goddess?

What her nymphs? Maidens?

What her pastimes? Hunting?

Telusa

A goddess? Who knows it not?
Maidens? Who thinks it not?
Hunting? Who loves it not?

Cupid

I pray thee, sweet wench, amongst all your sweet troop, is
there not one that followeth the sweetest thing, sweet love?

Telusa

Love, good sir, what mean you by it? Or what do you call
it?

Cupid

A heat full of coldness, a sweet full of bitterness, a pain full
of pleasantness, which maketh thoughts have eyes, and
hearts ears, bred by desire, nursed by delight, weaned by
jealousy, killed by dissembling, buried by ingratitude, and
this is love, lady, will you any?

Telusa

If it be nothing else, it is but a foolish thing.

Cupid

Try, and you shall find it a pretty thing.

Telusa

I have neither will nor leisure, but I will follow Diana in
the chase, whose maidens are all chaste, delighting in the
bow that wounds the swift hart in the forest, not fearing
the bow that strikes the soft heart in the chamber.

This difference is between my mistress Diana, and your
mother (as I guess) Venus, that all her nymphs are amiable
and wise in their kind, the other amorous and too kind for
their sex; and so farewell, little god.

Telusa *exits.* **Cupid** *rages.*

Cupid

Diana, and thou, and all thine, shall know that Cupid is a
great god!

I will practise a while in these woods, and play such pranks with these nymphs, that while they aim to hit others with their arrows, they shall be wounded themselves with their own eyes.

Exit.

Scene Three

Melebeus *and* **Phillida. Neptune** *and* **Venus** *watch*
[**Melebeus**, **Phillida** *and* **Neptune** *speak ENG.* **Venus** *speaks BSL.*]

Melebeus
Come, Phillida, beautiful Phillida, and I fear me too beautiful, being my Phillida. Thou knowest the custom of this country, and I the greatness of thy beauty, we both the fierceness of the monster Agar.

Everyone thinketh his own child special, but I know that which I most desire, and would least have: that thou art – special – and therefore shalt be sacrificed.

Thou shalt therefore disguise thy self in . . . attire, lest I should disguise myself in affection, in suffering thee to perish by a fond desire, whom I may preserve by a sure deceit.

Phillida
Dear Father, Nature could not make me so beautiful as she hath made you kind, nor you more kind than me dutiful. Whatsoever you command I will not refuse, because you command nothing but my safety, and your happiness. But how shall I be disguised?

Melebeus
In man's apparel.

Phillida
It will neither become my body, nor my mind.

Melebeus

Why, Phillida?

Phillida

For then I must keep company with boys, and commit
follies unseemly for my sex, or keep company with girls,
and be thought more wanton then becometh me. Besides,
I shall be ashamed of my long hose and short coat, and so
unwarily blab out something by blushing at everything.

Melebeus

Fear not, Phillida, use will make it easy, fear must make it
necessary.

Phillida

I agree, since my father will have it so, and fortune must.

Melebeus

Come let us in, and when thou art disguised, roam about
these woods till the time be past, and Neptune pleased.

Neptune *has been observing and is furious.*

*Perhaps as he speaks we see both sets of parent/child saying farewell
and* **Galatea** *and* **Phillida** *separately escaping.*

Neptune

Today should be the solemn sacrifice, wherein the
beautifullest maiden (were not the inhabitants faithless)
should be offered unto me, but so over-careful are parents
to their children, that they forget the safety of their
country, and fearing to become unnatural, become
unreasonable.

Their sleights may blear men, deceive me they cannot. I
will show as great cruelty as they have done craft, and well
shall you know that Neptune should have been entreated,
not cozened.

Now will I cause this river to rise and churn, the seas shall
break their bounds, the storms I keep bound up beneath
the earth shall be let loose and the land abused.

Do you think those fancy council flood defences are going to save you? Think again! I can broach them already!

As **Neptune** *speaks, the waters begin to rise around him.*

Beer kegs explode and a weather vane spins . . .

The storm-warning sirens begin to wail . . .

People from the town start running back and forwards towards the river –

'A flood! A storm! Quickly, quickly!'

Venus *comes over to* **Neptune** *and challenges what he is doing.*

Venus
What is this? Stop this chaos!

Neptune
They have disobeyed me

Venus
But all who journey on the water shall be wrecked, all who sail shall be lost?

Neptune
Then these mortals shall think twice before crossing me again.

Venus
You're being a massive prick

Neptune *rolls his eyes.*

Neptune
Ugh. fine. I'll see if I can save any of them – but next time no one shall be spared.

He goes off to become the **Mariner**.

Venus *rolls her eyes. She heads back to her area and watches the action.*

The storm continues.

Scene Four

Mariner *and* **Rafe**. **Hebe**.

Neptune (*disguised as the* **Mariner**) *has rescued* **Rafe**, *whose ship has been sunk in the storm.*

Hebe *is a volunteer immigration enforcement patrol officer who meets* **Rafe** *onshore.*

[**Hebe** *may speak BSL or ENG as feels appropriate – although* **Hebe** *is Deaf, they have been forced to assimilate into the hearing world.* **Rafe** *may speak/sign in multiple languages including ENG, BSL and ASL.* **Mariner** *speaks ENG.*]

Rafe *is being dragged ashore by the* **Mariner**. **Rafe** *is resisting, scrambling to go back for his missing brothers.* **Rafe** *is in shock – he has lost all of the people that he travelled with and is confused as to his location.*

Rafe (*in Filipino*)
  Iwanan mo ako! May Mga tao doon! [Leave me! There are still people there!]

Mariner (*firmly*)
  Come, thy safety first.

Rafe (*in Filipino*)
  Makinig ka! May mga tao! Hindi mo ba naiintindihan? May mga tao! [Listen! There's people! Do you not understand? There's people!] (*In English.*) There's people! People!

Mariner (*understanding the English*)
  Thy people, we will return to land later – for now, thy safety is utmost.

Rafe (*in English*)
  I was on a ship – we were on a ship – a lot of us.

Mariner
  A ship? Thou means a raft.

Rafe
  Raft? No, a / ship!

Hebe

/ An illegal raft.

Rafe

You do not understand me – not a raft, a ship –

Hebe

A 'ship', a 'raft', the time for thy stories comes after.

Rafe

I would rather hang myself on a rafter in the house, than be drowned in the sea; have you ever seen water churn as the sea did? We must find the others.

Hebe

I'll warrant by this time, they be drowned.

Rafe

But what shall I do?

Hebe

You are now in West Sussex, Little Shoreham /

Rafe

I –

Hebe

This town is a respectable one. There are woods hard by, and in that direction houses: so that if thou seeks on the land, thou shall speed better than on the sea.

Rafe (*signs in ASL*)

This is shit! (*Speaks in English.*) Sea? No, I will never sail again.

Rafe (*to* **Mariner**, *sarcastic*)

You have a sweet life, Mariner, to find safety in a few boards, and to be within an inch of some place bottomless. How often have you drowned?

Mariner

Fool, thou seest I am yet alive.

Rafe (*angry*)

Why, do those that drown die? I thought perhaps that the drowned were with the fish, and so could therefore be caught up with them in nets again. How can such little cold water kill a man of reason, when a poor minnow lies in it and has no understanding?

Mariner

Thou art wise from the crown of thy head upwards.

Hebe

The LSISSC, who I represent, offers help to those like you.

Rafe (*confusion*)

Like me?

Hebe (*signing, secretly, 'do not sign here'*)

Refugees.

Rafe

Refugees?

Hebe

As I told you, the time for the creation of your stories comes later. It is our civic duty . . . the Little Shoreham Immigration Services Support Committee. If one can help others, one should. (*Signing subtly.*) I can help you into the system. Help you get placed. Somewhere.

Rafe (*signs ASL and speaks*)

Help? Housed? With you?

Rafe *continues to attempt to interrupt* **Hebe** *in ASL/a mother language but their exhaustion grows.*

Hebe

No, I have no place for you – but you can be placed. In time. To begin, a waiting list in which one waits for initial approval for the process of administration, from that one waits to be assessed for assessment eligibility and advice on getting an adviser, of course we then must make checks on

your illegality, equitability and importantly integration.
You must wait here for the officials to arrive, who I will
contact – they shall get you into the system – assess
whether there is anywhere for you, if you belong? If you
are a threat. (*Signing subtly.*) Why did you come here?
What do you want from us?

Rafe (*exhausted*)
What do I want?

Hebe *leaves to summon the authorities.* **Rafe** *turns to the* **Mariner**
for help, but they are leaving too.

Mariner
Nay, I will follow mine old fortunes, and to sea again.

(*As* **Neptune**.)
I can shift the moon and the sun and stars. The wonders I
see would overload thine senses: I fear the sea no more
than a dish of water. Fools: it is but a liquid element.

(*As* **Mariner**.)
Farewell . . . seek you new fortunes . . . elsewhere.

He leaves.

Rafe (*to audience*)
I have neither means, nor plans, nor brothers; stripped
from my honesty now. I cannot send anything back, much
less bring it home. I do not even have a home.

He weighs up his options . . .

*He sings a mournful song – a prayer – he opens up to the audience
through it.*

(*Sings.*)
Rocks and sands and seas, farewell
Fie! Who would dwell in such a hell
This drunken ship we'll never quell
Yet dare to go and roam
Brave we are the fortuned few
To strive the beastly ocean blue

Pray for thy land's morning dew
Fight squalls and bring it back home
Up were we swallowed in wet graves
Soused in waves by Neptune's slaves
Toss'd to shore, our souls were saved
From monsters glutting bones
Brave we are the fortuned few
To strive the beastly ocean blue
Pray for thy land's morning dew
Fight squalls and bring it back home
We rove in kind or stormy weather
And as we live, we die together . . .
But they are drowned, my only brothers
I'll leave the seas unknown
Brave we are the fortuned few
To strive the beastly ocean blue
Pray for thy land's morning dew . . .
Fight squalls . . . and bring it back home

Rafe (*speaking*)
They are drowned, my brothers.

Pause.

Shall I go into the woods, and see what fortune I may
learn from the trees before they are made into ships? Or
go to the houses, before this churning sea turns them to
mud?

Rafe *sees hi-vis jackets on the way, makes a decision. He gestures to
the woods.*

I will this way . . . but let us all meet here again: it may be
that we shall either beg together, or hang together. It skills
not, so we be together.

Exeunt.

Rafe *moves into the woods/houses; perhaps he climbs over the fence
with the love knots . . .*

Act Two

Scene One

Enter **Galatea** *alone.*

They are uncomfortable in the clothes **Tityrus** *has picked for them – still smarting from losing the argument previously.*

Maybe they begin to 'accessorise or adapt' the clothes so they feel more real. **Galatea** *does not desire to 'be a boy', they just want to be themself.* [**Galatea** *speaks ENG.*]

Galatea

Blush, Galatea, that must frame thy affection fit for thy
habit, and therefore be thought immodest, because thou
art unfortunate.
O would the gods had made me as I seem to be, or that I
might safely be what I seem not.
My mum doesn't get it. She is letting her love for me
overtake her good judgement; I should be back there
fulfilling my destiny, not hiding in these woods!
But why dost thou blame her or blab what thou art, when
thou shouldst only counterfeit what thou art not.
But sssh, here comes a lad: I will learn of him how to
behave myself.

Enter **Phillida** *in 'man's attire'. She is profoundly uncomfortable.*
Galatea *hides themself – performing masculinity as they do.*
[**Phillida** *speaks ENG.*]

Phillida

I neither like my gait, nor my garments; the one
untoward, the other unfit – both unseemly.
O Phillida. But yonder stayeth one, and therefore say
nothing, but o Phillida!

During these next lines – they observe each other.

Galatea

From the way he is behaving, I perceive that boys are in as
great disliking of themselves as maids.

Therefore though I wear the apparel, I am glad I am not the person.

Phillida

He is a handsome boy, and pretty. He might well have been a woman, but because he is not, I am glad I am – for now, in my disguise, I shall decipher the follies of their kind.

Galatea

I would salute him, but I fear I should simper instead of swagger!

Phillida

If I trusted my face not to blush, I would spend some time to make pastime, for say what they will of a man's wit, it is no second thing to be a woman.

Galatea

Why stand I still? Boys should be bold . . . but here cometh a brave train that will spill all our talk.

The fence in front of **Diana**'s *camp breaks open and the woods spill out and overtake the set. We realise we are deep in the woods and here is the protest encampment of* **Diana** *and her nymphs. Refugees from the town, people who have chosen a life in the forest rather than a life of fear or danger.*

They left because they were scared, or because they were queer, or because they objected and they found her: **Diana** . . . *the Goddess of the Hunt, who taught them about her forest – how to live in nature, respect and revere it.*

They take only what they need and they live simply and peaceably – **Diana** *holds them tightly, but with respect.*

Enter **Diana** *followed by her train of* **Nymphs** *including* **Telusa**, **Eurota**, **Ramia** *and* **Larissa**. [**Diana** *is Deaf and speaks BSL. Her* **Nymphs** *are a mixture of Deaf and hearing and should speak accordingly.*]

As the **Nymphs** *surround* **Galatea** *and* **Phillida** *and take over the space, we see how awesome and disciplined they are.*

Diana
God speed, pretty boy.

Galatea
You are deceived, lady.

Diana
Why, are you no boy?

Galatea
No pretty boy.

Diana
But I see an unhappy boy.

Telusa
Saw you not the deer come this way; he flew down the wind, and I believe you have blanched him.

Galatea
Whose deer was it?

Telusa
Diana's deer.

Galatea (*to audience*)
I saw none but mine own dear. I know not how it commeth to pass, but yonder boy is in mine eye too beautiful; I pray gods these ladies think him not their dear . . .

Telusa (*to* **Diana**)
This wag is wanton or a fool, ask the other, Diana.

Diana (*to* **Phillida**)
Pretty lad, do you on purpose come to mar Diana's pastime?

Phillida (*lost*)
I understand not one word you speak.

Telusa (*to* **Diana**)

These boys are both agreed, either they are very pleasant or too perverse: you were best, lady, make them tusk these woods, whilst we stand with our bows, and so use them as beagles since they have so good mouths.

Diana

I will. Follow me without delay, or excuse, and if you can do nothing, yet shall you hallow the deer.

Phillida

I am willing to go, (*aside*) not for these ladies' company, because myself am a maiden, but for that boy's favour, who I think be a god.

Diana

You, sir boy, shall also go.

Galatea

I must if you command /

(*Aside.*)

/ and would if you had not.

They exit (or retreat into the camp). **Telusa** *remains on watch.*

Scene Two

Cupid *enters with* **Neptune** *listening.* **Cupid** *sneaks around* **Telusa** . . . *and uses controlling magic on her – waving their hand in* **Telusa**'s *face.*

Telusa *is puppet-ed by* **Cupid**, *who toys with her as they talk.*

Cupid *is not going to be humiliated.* [**Cupid** *and* **Neptune** *speak* ENG.]

Cupid

Now, Cupid, under the shape of a silly girl – show the power of a mighty god. Let Diana and all her coy nymphs know that there is no heart so chaste but thy bow can wound, nor eyes so modest, but thy brands can kindle, nor thoughts so staid, but thy shafts can make wavering, weak and wanton. Cupid, though he be young, is no baby.

Cupid *puts their sunglasses on* **Telusa**, *who is transformed by love. She goes into the audience and falls in love with everyone.*

Cupid

I will make their pains my pastimes, and so confound their loves, that they shall dote in their desires, delight in their affections, and practise only impossibilities.

Whilst I truant from my mother, I will use some tyranny in these woods!

And then, ladies, gentlemen and those clever enough to transcend the gender binary: if you see Diana's nymphs – yes, even Diana's nymphs! – entrapped in love, say softly to your selves, we may all love.

Cupid *calls* **Telusa** *back from the audience, and together they exit, in love.*

Neptune *is beginning to lose it. Does he speak this to* **Venus**?

Neptune

Not only do silly mortals go about to deceive great Neptune, in putting men's attire upon women: but Cupid (to make sport) deceives them all, by using a nymph's apparel upon a god?

Then Neptune, having often thrust thyself into the shape of beasts to deceive men be not coy to use the shape of a . . . member of the audience, to disguise thyself.

Neptune cannot be over-reached by swains, He is subtle, and if Diana be overtaken by this craft, Cupid is wiser than I thought. I will into these woods and mark all, and in the end will mar all.

Neptune *goes into the audience to observe! The woods continue to overtake the set as we see the chaos begin to fall out.*

Cupid *infecting the* **Nymphs** . . . *the committed band of activists and rebels is transformed into a chaotic hen party of lustful excess.*

Scene Three

Rafe *enters.* [**Rafe** *speaks ENG/signs ASL.*]

Rafe (*to audience*)

What is going on?! Are you watching the same thing I'm watching?

Call you this 'seeking of fortunes' when one can find nothing but birds' nests?

Would I were out of these woods, for I shall have but 'wooden' luck!

Here's nothing but the shrieking of owls, croaking of frogs, hissing of adders, barking of foxes. But, who comes here?

Enter the **Alchemist**'*s worker,* **Peter** [**Peter** *speaks ENG.*]

Peter *is gassing himself up to get through the work day. They know their shit and are putting in the work they've been instructed to do. When he's on his own, he's the expert in the room, a status he doesn't always have access to.*

Peter

Okay, Peter, you got this, baby, let's go! Let's get this bread, secure the bag – got some huffing and puffing to do, some mixing and matching, and best believe I know what I'm doing more than that daft old fart I work for!

While she talks about 'sublimation, almigation, calcination, rubification, circination, sementation, fermentation, encorporation, albification'

I'm working body magic . . .

transformation, modification, feminisation, maturation, metamorphoses, transition!

I seen her make potions that can change your destiny,
help people stay alive. But she works too slow,
pontificating on the past. I'm tryna freshen up the future,
focus on the things that people actually need.

Let's get into it, figure this out.

Peter *is setting up his kit to figure out how to make trans magic
potion.*

Rafe (*recognising a possible connection*)
I think this person may have what I need.

Peter (*impersonating the* **Alchemist**)
'Don't forget our instruments, crosslets, sublivatories,
cucurbits, limbecks, decensores, viols, manual and mural,
for imbibing and conbibing, bellows, molificative and
endurative. Then our metals, saltpetre, vitrioll, sal tartar,
sal perperat, argon, resagar, sal armonick, egrimony,
lumany, brimstone, valerian, tartar alam, breeme-wort,
glass, unsleked lime, chalk, ashes, hair'; and whatnot, to
make I know not what. (*He laughs*)

Rafe (*overhearing*)
What did he say? He's speaking a whole other language,
no?

Peter
So we go through this and that, do the most just to end up
with the least . . .

Rafe (*revealing himself to* **Peter**)
My day's been feeling about the same

Peter
Hello? Excuse me?

Rafe
You go through extremes to end with nothing, I'm just
saying that sounds like what I've been going through.

Peter (*bigging themself up*)
I dunno, it's not like I'm *not* getting anything out of this. I am an alchemist!

Rafe (*suspiciously*)
You? An alchemist?

Peter (*wrongly*) *assumes* **Rafe** *doesn't know what it means, and is excited to show off their knowledge* (*a total mansplainer!*)

Peter
I work for an alchemist . . . (*explaining*) AL-CHE-MIST . . . the magician . . . the legend!
She . . . and I, can make mysteries from the mundane, brilliance from the banal, turn worthless things into wonders.
Her art can cure an assortment of ailments. She . . . (*quickly*) and I channel ancestral knowledge from far before our times, and far beyond, spin secret sciences to retrieve treasures thieved. She . . . and I make ointments and potions to turn you into the best version of yourself, to give you strength or make you softer, to have you seen as you see yourself to be.
Through her work I've grown stronger and with surer sense of self, my jaw has set and my voice carries. That's more valuable to me than gold. But she's out here trying to make that too, if that's more your thing.

Rafe (*aside to the audience*)
Perhaps I could rest safely here, or even thrive . . . build myself up again?

He speaks to **Peter**.

If she . . . and you . . . can do that, she must be like a god?! With that intellect!

Peter (*scoffing – like she's not all that*)
When intellectuals are so enamoured in their thoughts that they forget their workers need to eat, I would wish for

an employer a touch less intelligent. Let me be real, it's not all roses here, a boss is a boss.

Rafe
Okay . . . but a job is a job, how can I get into this gig?

Peter
Okay, fine! I can teach you the basics. In our art we heal, we enrich. We change. There are spirits – the first spirit is quicksilver.

Rafe
I know about quicksilver, for my silver is so quick that I have much ado to catch it, and when I have it, it is so nimble, that I cannot hold it; I thought there was a spirit in it.

Peter (*laughs, in on the joke*)
The second spirit is fire. Brimstone.

Rafe
I know Brimstone too, a stinking spirit. I thought there was some spirit in it because it burnt so blue. My mother would often tell me that when the candle burnt blue, there was some ill spirit in the house, and now I perceive it was the spirit brimstone.

Peter
Ayy there you go! You got this! Okay and next, ingredients.
Have you ever had to get semen from a bull? First you gotta distract it really well/

Enter **Alchemist** *behind* **Peter** *who is oblivious, but* **Rafe** *becomes aware of the* **Alchemist**. [**Alchemist** *speaks ENG.*]

Peter (*carrying on*)
/ just watch out for the horns..

Alchemist *clears throat.* **Peter** *jumps, suddenly becoming meek and humbled.*

Alchemist

Who's this?

Peter

Someone keen to learn your craft. I was just telling . . . /?

Rafe

/ Rafe.

Peter

Rafe! What a genius you are!

Alchemist

Craft? You must call it a mystery.

Rafe

A mysterious craft or crafty mystery, it sounds good to me!

Alchemist

Can'st thou take pains?

Rafe

Infinite. But, I much marvel that you – being so cunning – should be so ragged.

Alchemist

O my child, griffins make their nests of gold though their coats are feathers, and we feather our nests with diamonds, though our garments be but simple. If thou knewest the secret of this science, the cunning would make thee so proud that thou wouldst disdain the outward pomp.

Peter (*conspiratorially*)

Mate, we work magic – but in this town it isn't smart for people like us to seem too comfortable. We are useful to have around but make them think you know your place . . .

Rafe

I have good fortune to light upon such a household!

Alchemist

When in the depth of my skill I determine to try the
uttermost of mine art, I am dissuaded by the gods,
otherwise, I would dare to make the fire as it flames into
gold, I would make the wind as it blows, silver, the water
as it runs, lead, I would make the earth as it stands, iron,
the sky, brass, and men's thoughts, firm metals.

Rafe

This art amazes me. And I'm no stranger to being
humbled by the gods.

Alchemist (*looks* **Rafe** *up and down carefully*)

You're not from here?

Rafe *nods.*

Tityrus *is intrigued – perhaps no one has arrived in this town
for many years. 'I see you . . .'*

Come in, and thou shalt see all.

Rafe

I follow, I run, I fly.

Alchemist *and* **Rafe** *exit.* **Rafe** *looks back at* **Peter** *as he leaves
and* **Peter** *gives him an encouraging thumbs-up.*

Peter

I am glad of this, for now I shall have leisure to run away;
this auntie's solidarity is stale . . . She's been here too long,
she thinks like one of them . . . treating those who work
for her as poorly as any of those old greybeards, let her
keep her new man, for she shall never see her old again; I
have what I need to go into business.
God shield me again, from blowing gold to nothing, with a
strong imagination to make nothing anything.

The chaos is building again – **Nymphs** *are running everywhere, in
love, in lust!* **Peter** *gets caught up in the chase, but isn't unhappy
about it . . . he quickly forgets his task as they enjoy the ride!*

Scene Four

Galatea *is alone – they have outrun the horny* **Nymphs**
for the time being . . . [*They speak in ENG.*]

Galatea

How now, Galatea? Miserable Galatea, that having put on
the apparel of a boy, thou canst not also put on the mind.
Had it not been better to have been a sacrifice to Neptune,
than a servant to Cupid? To die for thy country, than to
live in thy fancy? to be a sacrifice, than a lover?

O would when I hunted his eye with my heart, he might
have seen my heart with his eyes. Why did Nature to him,
a boy, give a face so beautiful? Or to me, a maiden, a
fortune so hard?

Well, I will swap my crochet for a bow . . . my soft ways for
something – harder? It may be, Galatea . . . (*are they gonna
admit something scary?*) foolish Galatea, what may be?
Nothing. Let me follow him into the woods, and thou,
sweet Venus, be my guide.

Galatea *exits.*

Venus *feels invoked and is watching both closely . . . Is this where
she becomes distracted by the lovers?*

Scene Five

Enter **Phillida** *alone.* [*She speaks ENG.*]

Phillida

Poor Phillida, curse the time of thy birth and rareness of
thy beauty, the unaptness of thy apparel, and the
untamedness of thy affections.

Art thou no sooner in the habit of a boy, but thou must be
enamoured of a boy?! What should I do, when what I
want the most, is what scares me the most of all?

O to openly be who I am with him could put me into danger; but being who I am not endangers this love yet to bloom. What choices are these?

I will go into the woods, watch the good times, his best moods, and transgress in love a little of my modesty. I will, I dare not. Thou must, I cannot. Then pine in thine own peevishness. I will not, I will. Ah, Phillida, do something, nay anything rather than live thus.

Well, what I will do, myself knows not, but what I ought I know too well, and so I go resolute, either to betray my love, or suffer shame.

Exit.

Act Three

Scene One

Enter **Telusa** *alone.* [*She signs in BSL.*]

She has been chasing **Galatea** *and* **Phillida**, *but has temporarily lost them.* **Telusa** *is wrestling with her own emotions and desires – she wants to stay loyal to* **Diana**'s *values, but is powerfully under* **Cupid**'s *spell.*

Telusa

How now? What new conceits, what strange contraries
breed in my mind? Is my Diana become a Venus?
O Telusa, these words are unfit for thy sex being a
maiden, but apt for thy affections being a lover.
And can there in vows so holy, in education so precise, and
in a heart so chaste, enter either a strong desire, or a wish,
or a wavering thought of love?
Can Cupid's brands quench Diana's flames, and his feeble
shafts headed with feathers, pierce deeper than Diana's
arrows headed with steel? I should break my bow because
I want to break my vow, and my hands that I normally use
for hunting should scratch out my eyes that have
wounded my heart.
O strange boy, because he is fine, must I be fickle, and
false my vow because I see his virtue?
Fond girl that I am to think of love, nay vain profession
that I follow to disdain love.
But here cometh Eurota; I must pretend to be normal.
Extremely normal! She mustn't see I am in love.

Telusa *fails at pretending to 'be normal'.*

Enter **Eurota**. [**Eurota** *may speak ENG or BSL as makes sense depending who they are speaking to.*]

Eurota

Telusa, Diana bid me hunt you out and says that you care
not to hunt with her, but if you follow any other game

than she hath roused, your punishment shall be to bend
all our bows, and weave all our strings. Why do you look
so strange?

Telusa *and* **Eurota** *play a game of 'Strange? I'm not strange!'*

Telusa (*breaking down*)
Eurota, the game I follow is the thing I fly: my strange
disease, my chief desire.

Eurota
Er, don't speak in riddles. I pray thee, Telusa, tell me
what's wrong with you?! If thou be sick, this ground hath
leaves to heal: if melancholy, here are pastimes to use: If
you are grumpy, we can give you jokes, time or advice . . .
If thou be in love (for I have heard of such a beast called
love) it shall be cured. Why blushest thou, Telusa?

Telusa
To hear thee in reckoning my pains to recite thine own. I
saw, Eurota, how amorously you glanced your eye on the
pretty boy in the woods, and how cunningly (now that you
would have some talk of love) you hit me in the teeth with
love.

Eurota (*breaking down*)
I confess that I am in love, and yet swear that I know not
what it is. I feel my thoughts unknit, mine eyes unstayed,
my heart I know not how affected, or infected, my sleeps
broken and full of dreams, my wakeness sad and full of
sighs, my self in all things unlike my self. If this be love, I
would it had never been devised.

Telusa
Thou hast told what I am in uttering what thy self is: these
are my passions, Eurota, my unbridled passions, my
intolerable passions!

Eurota
Ok, now we've both confessed . . . how did it take you first,
Telusa?!

Telusa

By the eyes, my wanton eyes, which conceived the picture of his face, and hanged it on the very strings of my heart. O fine boy! O fond Telusa. But how did it take you, Eurota?

Eurota

By the ears, whose sweet words sunk so deep into my head, so that even now I remember his wit and lose all of my wisdom . . .
O eloquent boy! O credulous Eurota!
But, soft, here comes Ramia. But let them not hear us talk; we will withdraw ourselves, and hear them talk.

Enter **Ramia**.

Eurota *and* **Telusa** *hide.* [**Ramia** *may speak ENG or BSL as makes sense depending who they are speaking to.*]

Ramia

I am sent to seek others that am lost myself.

Eurota (*watching* **Ramia**)

You shall see Ramia hath also bitten on a love leaf.

Ramia

Can there be no heart so chaste, but love can wound? Nor vows so holy but affection can violate? Vain art thou virtue, and thou chastity but a byword, when you both are subject to love, of all things the most abject. If love be a god, why should not lovers be virtuous?! Love is a god, and lovers are virtuous!

Eurota (*revealing herself*)

Indeed, Ramia, if lovers were not virtuous, then wert thou vicious.

Ramia

What, are you come so near me?

Telusa

I think we came near you when we said you loved.

Eurota

Tush, Ramia, 'tis too late to recall it, to repent it a shame: therefore, I pray thee, tell what is love?

Ramia

If it was only me who were in love, I would be happy to come up with a dictionary definition, but so many people are in love that I would not dare to take this responsibility. But let's all talk about that later. Diana was losing it, because she keeps sending one more person to seek the last, and now she's running out of nymphs!

Everyone is grovelling and falling at the feet of the strange boys in the woods. Even I, and I blush to admit it, am obsessed with that boy, that pretty boy, that beautiful boy.

Telusa

What have we here, all in love? No other food than fancy; no, no, she shall not have the boy.

Eurota

Nor you, Telusa.

Ramia

Nor you, Eurota.

They fight.

Telusa

I love the boy, and my deserts shall be answerable to my desires. I will forsake Diana for him. I will die for him.

Ramia

I love him!

Eurota

So do I, and I will have him.

They fight.

Telusa

Immodest all that we are, unfortunate all that we are like to be. Shall maidens begin to wrangle for love, and become wanton in their thoughts, in their words, in their actions?

O divine love, which art therefore called divine, because thou over-reachest the wisest, conquerest the chastest, and doeth all things both unlikely and impossible, because thou art love. Thou makest the bashful impudent, the wise fond, the chaste wanton, and workest contraries to our reach, because thy self is beyond reason.

Eurota

Talk no more, Telusa, your words wound. Ah, would I were no woman.

Ramia

Would there were no boy.

Telusa

Would I were no body.

Cupid *has been watching and laughing at the scene.*

Galatea *and* **Phillida** *are discovered again by the* **Nymphs** *who chase them again and end up beneath the lovers – the BSL-speaking actors partly translating the lovers' next scene to each other and falling in love with each other at the same time!*

These two scenes should exist in harmony with each other, but can be completely separate.

Scene Two

Phillida *and* **Galatea**. [*Speaking ENG.*]

Phillida *and* **Galatea** *are unaware that they are being observed by two of* **Diana**'s **Nymphs**. *The* **Nymphs** *try to understand their conversation to avoid being caught. They keep their distance and change their point of view whenever* **Phillida** *and* **Galatea** *suspect they are being watched.*

Venus *observing and involved with this.*

Phillida

It is pity that Nature framed you as a boy, having a face so
beautiful, so lovely a countenance, so modest a behaviour.

Galatea

There is a tree in Tylos, whose nuts have shells like fire,
and being cracked, the kernel is but water.

Phillida

What a toy is it to tell me of that tree, being nothing to the
purpose: I say it is pity you are a boy.

Galatea

I would not wish to be a woman, unless it were because
thou art a man.

Phillida

Neither me, for then I should not love thee, for I have
sworn never to love a woman.

Galatea

A strange humour in so pretty a youth, and according to
mine, for myself will never love a woman.

Phillida

It were a shame if a maiden should be a suitor, that thou
shouldst deny to be her servant.

Galatea

If it be a shame in me, it can be no commendation in you,
for yourself is of that mind.

Phillida

Suppose I were a maiden (I blush in supposing myself
one) and that under the habit of a boy were the person of
a maid, if I should utter my affection with sighs, manifest
my sweet love by my salt tears, and prove my loyalty
unspotted, and my griefs intolerable, would not then that
beautiful face pity this true heart?

Galatea

Admit that I were, as you would have me suppose that you
are, and that I should with entreaties, prayers, oaths,

bribes, and whatever can be invented in love, desire your favour, would you not yield?

Phillida
Tush, you come in with admit.

Galatea
And you with suppose.

Phillida (*to audience*)
What doubtful speeches be these? I fear me he is as I am, a maiden.

Galatea (*to audience*)
What dread riseth in my mind; I fear the boy to be as I am, a maiden.

Phillida (*to audience*)
Tush, it cannot be, his voice shows the contrary.

Galatea (*to audience*)
Yet I do not think it, for he would then have blushed.

Phillida
Have you ever a sister?

Galatea
If I had but one my brother must needs have two; but I pray have you ever a one?

Phillida
My father had but one daughter, and therefore I could have no sister.

Galatea
Ay me, he is as I am, for his speeches be as mine are.

Phillida
What shall I do, either he is subtle or I am simple.

Galatea (*to audience*)
I have known diverse of Diana's nymphs enamoured of him, yet hath he rejected all, either as too proud to disdain, or too childish not to understand, or for that he knoweth himself to be a maiden.

Phillida (*to audience*)
I am in a quandary; Diana's nymphs have followed him,
and he despised them, either knowing too well the beauty
of his own face, or that himself is of the same mould. I will
once again try him.

(*To* **Galatea**.)
You promised me in the woods that you would love me
before all Diana's nymphs.

Galatea
Ay, so you would love me before all Diana's nymphs.

Phillida
Can you prefer a fond boy as I am, before so pretty ladies
as they are?

Galatea
Why should not I as well as you?

Phillida
Come, let us into the grove, and make much of one
another, that cannot tell what to think of one another.

Exeunt.

Venus *acknowledges she doesn't need to see this . . . She leaves!*

Venus
I think they can handle things from here! And you lot? I'll
see you later.

She blows a kiss.

Scene Three

Alchemist (**Tityrus**) *and* **Rafe**. [*The* **Alchemist** *speaks ENG.*
Rafe *signs ASL/speaks ENG as feels right.*]

Alchemist
Rafe! My apprentice, Peter, is run away. I trust thou wilt
not run after?

Rafe

I would I had a pair of wings that I might fly after.

Alchemist

Why, thou hast not yet seen the end of my art!

Rafe

I would I had not known the beginning. You promised me, that of my silver necklace – you would make a whole cupboard full! But when we put it in the flames, it just melted to nothing! That belonged to my father – it was all I had . . .

Alchemist

Rafe, the fortune of this art consisteth in the measure of the fire, for if there be a coal too much, or a spark too little, if it be a little too hot, or a thought too soft, all our labour is in vain.

Besides, they that blow must beat time with their breaths, as musicians do with their breasts, so as there must be of the metals, the fire and workers a very harmony.

Rafe

Nay, if you desire to be in harmony with your workers, you must join them. You see yourself above me – never in collaboration but shrouded in supremacy. You treat me as a parent might treat a child. Did you ever ask me what I know already? How I could have helped? What I can do? Nobody asks.

Alchemist

I promise that if you work hard for me, often it does happen. When the just proportion of the fire and all things concur.

Rafe

Concur? Condog. I will away.

Alchemist

Then away! . . . Everyone has gone away . . .

Exit **Alchemist**.

Enter **Journalist** (**Melebeus**) *and* **Hebe**. [**Journalist**, **Rafe** *and* **Hebe** *may speak BSL or ENG.*]

Rafe
A job, where you make so much in the day, that you have nothing to buy food with come the night?

Journalist
Sounds like you have a story here, boy. Can you give me a statement? . . . Son? Care to make a comment? For my show, 'Shoreham Today'?

Rafe *looks alarmed.* **Journalist** *starts writing/dictating to* **Hebe***:*

Hebe *on tablet, writing the banner headlines:*

WAGE DISPUTE – WORKERS ON STRIKE (AGAIN)
or
TROUBLE BREWING

Rafe (*signs to* **Hebe** *in ASL*)
What are you doing?

Journalist
Predicting the future.

Rafe
Predicting?

Journalist *looks smug.*

Journalist
I write the future, boy . . . It's whatever I want it to be.

Rafe
I'm not a boy . . . and fortune telling is a scam.

Journalist *notices the criticism, notes that* **Rafe** *is different/new/a potential target . . . but doesn't say anything.* **Journalist** *signs 'Tell him'.*

Hebe
There is (*ASL fingerspells integrity*) integrity in this work.

Rafe *corrects* **Hebe** *with the ASL sign for 'integrity'.*

Journalist

We are truth tellers . . . predictors, forecasters even.

Do you not want to control your own narrative? Do you
not know the power that lies in being the one who tells the
stories, who holds the pen? People across this land heed
my words and take them into their hearts. I tell people
what is important right now, what to care about. This town
would lose itself otherwise.

Hebe

You cannot have people running around not knowing
what to think, that would create absolute chaos!

Journalist

It's vital to have someone, like me, keeping everything in
check.

Do you understand this power? What is broadcast is what
will be. The words I speak become truth. So go on, give
me a statement, just a few words.

Rafe (*aside to themself*)

I know kinds of men like him. But he says people across
this land heed his words . . . Perhaps, if I can tell my story
. . .

(*To* **Journalist**.)

Whoever holds the truth holds the power. I could give you
my story, but I could tell it myself it too – Let me work
with you, learn your craft.

Journalist

I accept. Come and tell me your tale –

As they exit **Journalist** *spells* (*signs*) *out a headline behind* **Rafe**'s
back:

'Exclusive Interview: THE MIGRANT MONSTER.'

Scene Four

Diana *is asleep/resting in her caravan.*

Telusa, **Eurota**, **Ramia**, **Larissa** *and other* **Nymphs** *arrive intoxicated with love –* **Cupid** *disguised among them.* **Peter** *is having the time of their life amongst them all. They all arrive singing* **Nymphs**, *'Love Song'.* [**Diana** *speaks BSL – other characters speak/sign as appropriate.*]

Nymphs (*sing*)
How did love take you?
It took me by the eyes.
I hung a picture of his face on the strings of my heart

How did love take you?
It took me by the ears
With his sweet words sunk deep into my head

It felt like an infection
Without a definition
I cannot describe it
And now I feel so shameless
Love conquers innocence
It feels impossible to fight it

They attempt to be quiet, but clumsily awake **Diana** *who rebukes them.*

Diana
What news have we here, ladies, are all in love?

Are Diana's nymphs become Venus's wantons? Is it a shame to be chaste, because you be amiable? Or must you needs be amorous, because you are beautiful?

O Venus, if this be thy spite, I will requite it with more than hate; well shalt thou know what it is to drib thine arrows up and down Diana's leas.
Now, nymphs, ladies, doth not that make your cheeks blush, that makes mine ears glow? Or can you remember that without sobs, which Diana can not think on without

sighs? What greater dishonour could happen to Diana, or
to her nymphs' shame, than that there can be any time so
idle, that should make their heads so addle?

She gives examples which become illustrated behind her . . .

Your chaste hearts, my nymphs, should resemble the
Onyx, which is hottest when it is glows; and your
thoughts, the more they are assaulted with desires, the less
they should be affected.

It was a bad example . . . She tries again.

You should think love like a plant, its leaves look beautiful
but its roots taste terrible, a spectacular show and a bitter
taste.

It is a better example, but she still hasn't nailed it . . .

Of all trees the cedar is greatest, and hath the smallest
seeds: of all affections, love hath the greatest name, and
the least virtue.

That was a good one!

Shall it be said, and shall Venus say, that Diana, the
Goddess of Chastity, whose thoughts are always
answerable to her vows, whose eyes never glanced on
desire, and whose heart abateth the point of Cupid's
arrows, shall have her maidens to become unchaste in
desires, immoderate in affection, untemperate in love, in
foolish love, in base love.

O, my dear nymphs, if you knew how loving thoughts
stain lovely faces, you would be as careful to have the one
as unspotted as the other beautiful.

Cast before your eyes the loves of Venus's trulls, their
fortunes, their fancies, their ends.

And how is your love placed? Upon pelting boys! Perhaps
base of birth, without doubt weak of discretion!

She is making fun of them.

'Aye, but they are pretty'. O, nymphs, do your eyes begin
to love colours, whose hearts were wont to loathe them? Is
Diana's chase become Venus's court? And are your holy
vows turned to hollow thoughts?

Telusa

Madam, if love were not a thing beyond reason, we might
then give a reason of our doings, but so divine is his force,
that it works effects contrary to that we wish, as
unreasonable against that we ought.

Eurota

Lady, so unacquainted are we with the passions of love,
that we can neither describe them nor bear them.

Diana

Foolish nymphs, how willing you are to follow that which
you should fly.

As she speaks, she moves behind the **Nymphs** – *inspecting them . . .*

There is an unknown nymph that straggleth up and down
these woods, which I suspect hath been the weaver of
these woes. I saw them slumbering by the brookside.

If you find upon their shoulder a burn, it is Cupid:
If any print on their back like a leaf, it is Medea:
If any picture on their left breast like a bird, it is Calipso.

She finds **Cupid***'s burn* (*tattoo*).

Diana

How now, sir, are you caught, are you Cupid?

Cupid

Thou shalt see, Diana, that I dare confess myself to be
Cupid.

Diana *grows and changes in her powerful wrath – she shows herself
as a goddess.*

Diana (*supported by nymphs in song*)

I am conqueror of your loose and untamed impulses
And thou shalt see, Cupid, that I will show myself to be,

Myself to be Diana
Did your mother Venus send thee to wound?
As for you Cupid
Venus has canes that are made from roses
Diana has canes made of thorns
I will teach thee, Cupid,
I will teach thee,
I will break thy bow,
And burn thy arrows
I will bind thy hands
Fetter thy feet
And clip thy wings
I will teach thee
Thou shall feel the smart of Diana
Let Venus, that great goddess, ransom Cupid, little god

These nymphs here whom thou hast infected with foolish love, shall both tread on thee and triumph over thee.

I will teach thee what it is to displease Diana, distress her nymphs, or disturb her game.

Cupid

Diana, what I have done, cannot be undone, but what you mean to do, shall. Venus hath some gods to her friends; Cupid shall have all.

Diana

Are you serious? I will bridle thy tongue and thy power. Do you think your mother is going to come and save you? Keep dreaming.
I'll show you I'm in charge here.

She gestures to her nymphs.

Eurota

We will plague you for a little god.

Telusa

We will never pity thee though thou be a god.

Ramia

Nor I.

Larissa

Nor I.

They sing and as they sing they destroy **Cupid**'s *wings.*

O yea, o yea, if any maid,
Who leering Cupid has betrayed
To frowns of spite, to eyes of scorn,
And would in madness now see torn
The boy in pieces, let her come
Hither, and lay on him her doom
O yea, o yea, has any lost
A heart which many a sigh hath cost,
Is any cozened of a tear,
Which (as a pearl) disdain does wear?
Here stands the thief, let her but come
Hither, and lay on him her doom.
Is anyone undone by fire,
And turned to ashes through desire?
Did ever any lady weep,
Being cheated of her golden sleep?
Stolen by sick thoughts! The pirate's found,
And in her tears, he shall be drowned
Read his indictment, let him hear,
What he's to trust to: boy, give ear!

Interval act.

During the interval, while the audience are getting drinks and stretching their legs, the **Nymphs** *put* **Cupid** *to work untying the love knots left at the beginning of the show. This should have the feel of a cabaret act, loose and free – the actors can divert from the script as they wish and audience play is encouraged.*

NB: the text here is a guide only!

[**Telusa** *speaks BSL.* **Cupid**, **Ramia**, **Eurota** *speak BSL/ENG as appropriate.*]

Telusa

Come, Cupid, to your task. First, you must undo all these lovers' knots, because you tied them.

Cupid

If they be true love knots, 'tis unpossible to unknit them; if false, I never tied them.

Eurota

Make no excuse but to it.

Cupid

Love knots are tied with eyes, and cannot be undone with hands, made fast with thoughts, and cannot be unloosed with fingers; had Diana no task to set Cupid to but things impossible,

Cupid *is actually making them even tighter.*

Ramia

Why, how now? You tie the knots faster!

Cupid

I cannot choose; it goeth against my mind to make them loose.

Eurota *tries to undo one.*

Eurota

Let me see, now 'tis unpossible to be undone.

Cupid

It is the true love knot of a woman's heart, therefore cannot be undone.

Ramia

That one falls apart in pieces . . .

Cupid

It was made of a cis man's thought, which will never hang together.

Cupid *unties another.*

Ramia
You have undone that well.

Cupid
Aye, because it was never tied well.

Telusa
These two knots are finely untied.

Cupid
It was because I never tied them: the one was knit by money, not love; the other by force, not faith.

Cupid *puts one aside.*

Ramia
Why do you lay that knot aside?

Cupid
For death.

Telusa
Why?

Cupid
Because the knot was knit by faith, and must only be unknit of death.

Cupid *laughs at one that is really extravagant.*

Eurota
Why laugh you?

Cupid
Because it is the finest and the falsest, done with greatest art and least truth, with best colours, and worst conceits.

Telusa
Who tied it?

Cupid
A teenager!

Cupid *gives one to* **Larissa**.

Larissa

Why do you put that in my bosom?

Cupid

Because it is only for a woman's bosom.

Larissa

Why, what is it?

Cupid

A woman's heart.

End of interval.

When the signal is given that the interval is over:

Telusa

Come let us go in, and tell that Cupid hath done his task. Stay you behind, Eurota, and see he sleep not, for love will be idle, and take heed you partake not, for love will be wanton.

Exit **Telusa**.

Cupid

Lady, can you for pity see Cupid thus punished?

Eurota

Why did Cupid punish us without pity?

Cupid

Is love a punishment?

Eurota

It is no pastime.

Cupid

O, Venus (Mummy), if thou sawest Cupid as a captive, bound to obey that was wont to command, fearing ladies' threats, that once pierced their hearts, I cannot tell whether thou wouldst revenge it for despite, or laugh at it for disport.

The time may come, Diana, and the time shall come, that thou that settest Cupid to undo knots, shall entreat Cupid

to tie knots, and you, ladies, that with solace have beheld
my pains, shall with sighs entreat my pity.

Enter **Ramia.**

Ramia

Come, Cupid, Diana hath devised new labours for you
that are God of Love.

You shall weave samplers all night, and lackey after Diana
all day.

You shall shortly shoot at beasts for men, because you have
made beasts of men, and wait on ladies' trains, because
thou entrappest ladies by trains.

Every tale of love, you must pick out with your needle,
and in that place sew Diana with her nymphs. How like
you this, Cupid?

Cupid

I say I will prick as well with my needle, as ever I did with
mine arrows.

Telusa

Diana cannot yield; she conquers affection.

Cupid

Diana shall yield; she cannot conquer destiny.

Eurota

Come, Cupid, you must to your business.

Cupid

You shall find me so busy in your heads, that you shall
wish I had been idle with your hearts.

Exeunt.

Act Four

Scene One

Neptune, Melebeus, Tityrus, Hebe, Townspeople. [**Neptune** *and* **Tityrus** *speak ENG.* **Melebeus** *and* **Hebe** *speak ENG/BSL.*]

We are back in the town square, as in the beginning of the show . . .
We have not been here for a while. The townspeople, once
resplendent in their Neptune Day outfits, are now sheepish and
worried. Things are going very badly wrong – the atmosphere has
turned sour.

Neptune

This is the day wherein you must satisfy Neptune and save
yourselves. Call together your daughters, and for this
sacrifice take the finest, for better it is to offer a maiden
than suffer ruin.

If you think it against nature to sacrifice your children,
think it also against sense to destroy your country. If you
imagine Neptune pitiless to desire such a prey, confess
yourselves perverse to deserve such a punishment.
You see this circle, this fatal ring, whose stones, though
ancient, threateneth to maidens' grief. In this place must
the most beautifullest be bound until the monster Agar
carry her away, and if the monster come not, then assure
yourselves that the finest is concealed, and then your
country shall be destroyed.

Therefore consult with yourselves, not as parents of
children, but as favourers of your country. Let Neptune
have his right if you will have your quiet; thus have I
warned you to be careful, and would wish you to be wise,
knowing that who so hath the finest daughter, hath the
greatest fortune, in losing one to save all. And so I depart
to enjoy ceremonies for the sacrifice, and command you to
bring the sacrifice.

Exit **Neptune**.

*The town is tense . . . Why has the sacrifice not been found? It
doesn't normally go like this!*

Melebeus *and* **Tityrus** *are shifty . . . nervous.*

Melebeus
They say, Tityrus, that you have a dutiful daughter, if it be
so, lie not, for you shall be a fortunate mother. It is a thing
holy to preserve one's country, and honourable to be the
cause.

Tityrus
Indeed, Melebeus, I have heard you boast that you had a
daughter, of which none was more beautiful. I hope you
are not so careful of a child, that you will be careless of
your country.

Melebeus
I must confess that I had a daughter, and I know you
have, but alas my child's cradle was her grave. I would she
had lived 'til now, she should willingly have died now; for
what could have happened to poor Melebeus more
comfortable, than to be the father of a fortunate child and
sweet country.

Tityrus
O, Melebeus, dissemble you may with me, deceive the
gods you cannot. Did not I see (and very lately see) your
daughter sneaking away from town? You have conveyed
her away, that you might cast us all away.

Melebeus
How dare you?! Who even are you? You make the people
believe that you wish well, when you practise nothing but
ill, wishing to be thought religious towards the gods, when
I know you are deceitful towards men.

Tityrus
You cannot over-reach me, Melebeus, overshoot yourself
you may. It is a wily mouse that will breed in the cat's ear.

Melebeus

Did you ever see me with my daughter? You are deceived; it was my son. But it matters not, *you* have a fair daughter, Tityrus, and it is pity you are so fond.

Tityrus

Call you my child fair? Your daughter a son? For shame.

Hebe

You are both either too confused or too contrary: for whilst you dispute to save your children, we neglect to prevent our destruction.

Another Townsperson

Come, let us away and seek out another sacrifice.

Exeunt.

Scene Two

Enter **Galatea** *and* **Phillida**. [*They speak ENG.*]

Galatea

I marvel what maiden the people will present for the sacrifice? It is happy you are none, for then it would have fallen to your lot . . . because you are so beautiful.

Phillida

But if you had been a maiden, too, I need not have feared – because you are more beautiful.

Galatea

I pray thee, sweet one, flatter not me; speak truth of thyself, for in mine eye of all the world thou art most beautiful.

Phillida

These be beautiful words, but far from thy true thoughts. I know my own face in a true glass, and desire not to see it in a flattering mouth.

Galatea

Seeing we are both boys, and both lovers, that our
affection may have some show, and seem as it were love,
let me call thee mistress.

Phillida

I accept that name, for diverse before have called me
mistress.

Pause.

Will you not be at the sacrifice?

Galatea

No.

Phillida

Why?

Galatea

Because I dreamt that if I were there, I should be turned
to a maiden, and then being so beautiful (as thou sayst I
am) I should be offered, as thou knowest one must. But
will not you be there?

Phillida

Not unless I were sure that a boy might be sacrificed, and
not a maiden.

Galatea

Why then you are in danger.

Phillida

But I would escape it by deceit. But seeing we are resolved
to be both absent, let us wander into these groves, 'til the
hour be past.

Galatea

I am agreed, for then my fear will be past.

Phillida

Why, what dost thou fear?

Galatea

Nothing but that you love me not.

Exit.

Phillida

I do. Poor Phillida, what shouldst thou think of thyself, that lovest one that, I fear me, is as thyself is; and may it not be that their parent practised the same deceit with them, that my father hath with me, and knowing them apt to be picked for sacrifice, feared they should be unfortunate.

If it be so, Phillida, how desperate is thy case? If it be not, how doubtful? For if she be a maiden, there is no hope of my love; if a boy, a hazard: I will after him or her, or them, and lead a melancholy life, that look for a miserable death.

Exit.

Act Five

Scene One

Enter **Rafe**. [**Rafe** *signs ASL or speaks ENG.*]

Rafe

No more masters now. A journalist?! Of all occupations
that's the worst. At least the alchemist keeps good fires
though she gets no gold; the other stands warming
himself by lying about people, lies that I think he sooner
can concoct than could conceive their virtues.

But hold on, is not this Peter?

Enter **Peter**.

Peter

What, Rafe? Well met. No doubt you had a warm service
of the alchemist?

Rafe

'Twas warm indeed, for the fire almost burnt out my eyes,
and yet my teeth still watered with hunger: so that my
service was both too hot and too cold. But where have you
been since?

Peter

Listen, it has been fully wild out here – I thought I was
gonna figure this alchemy gig and then I got caught in
this hectic party and it got weird . . . Diana showed up and
. . . Still, I'm sorry! I did try and warn you about the
alchemist . . .

Rafe

Looks like you had more fun than I did! It was not only
her under whom I was exploited. This journalist –
Melebeus / took me in

Peter

/ Yo, I know that guy, he's a nightmare! Are you okay? But
honestly – in this town they're all different versions of the

same mistreatment. There's no such thing as a just job!
I'm sick of it.

Peter *has a thought – what if he teamed up with* **Rafe***?*

I thought I'd be able to go make it on my own but my own
isn't enough.

Rafe
There's more of us than them, you know.

Enter **Galatea** *and* **Phillida***. As they all meet, the scene has lots of
excitement, confusion, talking over each other.*

Galatea
Oh, look it's Peter, he works for my mum / – Peter!

Phillida
/ Your mum?

Peter (*to* **Galatea**)
Eyyyy. Alright, kid, what's going on here? Thought I'd
run into you sometime soon!

Galatea
Did Mum send you? Is it over?

Peter
Ahh . . . no. I . . . left.

Rafe
This is the alchemist's child?

Galatea
Who are you?

Rafe
I'm Rafe.

Galatea
Galatea. And this is my . . . er, my friend. We just met . . .
This is Phillida –

Phillida
Hey, Peter!

Peter
Hey, hun!

Galatea *looks between* **Phillida** *and* **Peter**, *confused.*

Galatea
You know each other?

Peter
Yeah, you come to get your 'mones from the Alchemist, innit?

Galatea *gets excited.*

Galatea
What?! That's my mum! How come I've never seen you? Imagine if our paths had crossed in the past and we didn't even / know!

Phillida
So wild.

Galatea (*laughing*)
/ Imagine if I had been in the company of your parents without you knowing?

Phillida
I'd rather not.

Peter
Her dad's that bloke off the TV

Rafe
The journalist?

Galatea
That's your dad? But he hates people like us?!

Phillida
It's complicated. Don't hate me. This . . . this time away from him, with you, I feel more myself than I've been able to before.

Rafe

Your father told me a long tale of 'integrity' and 'truth',
whilst in the same breath saying 'balanced debate' and
'moral outrage'. He said he was like a soothsayer of sorts, a
predictor, a forecaster . . . reading signs to untangle the
truth and publish it. In the meantime he fell backward
into the river.

Peter

Did you ask him why he foresaw not that if he could write
the future?!

Rafe

He said he knew it, but held it in contempt. Every time he
opens his mouth, there is a waft of lies to endure.

Phillida

My dad fell in the river?! That is so embarrassing.

Rafe (*to* **Galatea**)

And with your mother, I had short shrift also – there I
melted all my meat, but created only disturbed thoughts,
and so had a full head and an empty belly.

Galatea

That sounds about right.

Peter (*with a tinge of sadness*)

You must miss her though? Have you thought about how
it's gonna be going home?

Peter *gives* **Galatea** *a once-over, grinning. Noting some change.*
Galatea *gets self-conscious, aware of their new-found identity.*

Galatea (*gender angst, thoughtful*)

I don't know . . .

(*To* **Phillida**.)

Are you going home?

Phillida

I suppose so?

Peter
Ohhh, you two! Come on, we'll just have to have each
other's back. We'll figure it out together, we'll figure it all
out – the sacrifice must be done by now, we'll just go and
take it all step by step, yeah?

Galatea
Are you coming back then?

Peter
I think so. I thought I had everything I needed out here,
but there's been something missing.

I forgot that from unusual relationships can come family,
and that a family is just as maddening and inconsiderate
as they are a solace and devotion. I see you as a sibling,
and Tityrus as a mother.
Return, I must.

How about it, Rafe? Do you want to try and reform that
grumpy old fool?

Rafe
Reform? No. But collaborate with you . . . I'd like to stick
around.

Peter
I'd like that.

They exit.

Scene Two

Neptune *and* **Melebeus**. [*They speak in ENG.*]

Neptune
Bring forth the maiden, the fatal maiden, the chastest
maiden, if you mean to appease Neptune, and preserve
your country.

Melebeus
Here she cometh.

Enter **Hebe**, *led by townspeople to be the sacrifice. They are chained to the ground.* [**Hebe** *speaks BSL.*]

Now all withdraw, because it is a sight unseemly to see the misfortune of a maiden, and terrible to behold the fierceness of Agar that monster.

Hebe

Miserable and accursed Hebe, that being neither young nor fortunate, thou shouldst be thought most happy and beautiful.

Curse thy birth, thy life, thy death, being born to live in danger, and having lived, to die by deceit.

Am I the sacrifice to appease Neptune, and satisfy the custom, the bloody custom, ordained for the safety of thy country?

Aye, Hebe, poor Hebe, men will have it so, whose forces command our weak natures; nay, the gods will have it so, whose powers dally with our purposes.

But, alas, destiny alloweth no dispute, die Hebe, Hebe die, woeful Hebe, and only accursed Hebe.

Farewell the sweet delights of life, and welcome now the bitter pangs of death.

Farewell to the maiden Hebe,
She who worshipped Neptune,
Farewell to Hebe who was always well dressed and pretty,
Who behaved how you wanted her to behave in order to win your affections.

Farewell, you chaste maidens, whose thoughts are divine, whose faces pretty, whose fortunes are agreeable to your affections. Enjoy and long enjoy the pleasure of your curled locks, the amiableness of your wished looks, the sweetness of your tuned voices, the content of your inward thoughts, the pomp of your outward shows.

I no longer must pretend to be like you. I am no maiden.

No longer Hebe. (*Signs old sign name.*)
But instead . . . Hebe (*signs new sign name*) shall be themself.

I honour the sovereign of all virtue, and goddess of all maidens, Diana, whose perfections are impossible to be numbered, and therefore infinite, never to be matched, and therefore immortal.

But alas, Hebe, thou art too late. And so, farewell, Diana too.

How happy had I been if I had not been. Farewell life, vain life, wretched life, whose sorrows are long, whose end doubtful, whose miseries certain, whose hopes innumerable, whose fears intolerable.

Come death, and welcome death whom nature cannot resist, because necessity ruleth, nor defer because destiny hasteth.

Come, Agar, thou unsatiable monster of maidens' blood, and devourer of beauty's bowels. Glut thy self 'til thou surfeit, and let my life end thine. Tear these tender joints with thy greedy jaws, this fearful face with thy foul teeth.

Why abatest thou thy wonted swiftness? Come, Agar, thou horrible monster, and farewell world, thou viler monster.

The monster does not come.

Neptune *leaves without saying a word . . . Silently steaming.*

Melebeus
The monster is not come, and therefore I see Neptune is abused, whose rage will, I fear me, be both infinite and intolerable: take in this maiden, whose want of virtue hath saved her own life, and stolen all yours.

Townsperson
We could not find anyone better.

Melebeus

Neptune will.

They exit.

Hebe

Fortunate Hebe, how shalt thou express thy joys?
Nay, unhappy Hebe, that hath not been the most virtuous.
Had it not been better for thee to have died with fame,
than to live with dishonour?
But alas, destiny would not have it so, destiny could not. I
would Hebe thou hadst been more virtuous.

Exeunt

Hebe *is left alone – where will they go?! They make a choice – they
have a second chance and they're gonna try their luck with* **Diana**
and the **Nymphs***! Nervously,* **Hebe** *heads towards* **Diana***'s camp,
passing the lovers on the way.*

Scene Three

Phillida, **Galatea**, **Rafe** *and* **Peter**. [*They speak ENG.*]

Phillida

Was Hebe the maiden that should have been offered to
Neptune? Belike either the custom is pardoned, or she not
thought best.

Galatea

I cannot conjecture the cause, but I fear the event.

Rafe

But soft, what man or god is this? Let us closely withdraw
ourselves into the thickets.

Enter **Neptune** *alone.* [**Neptune** *speaks ENG.*]

Neptune

And do men begin to be equal with gods, seeking by craft
to over-reach me, when I by power over-see them?
Do they dote so much on their daughters, that they stick

not to dally with our deities? Well shall the inhabitants see, that destiny cannot be prevented by craft, nor my anger be appeased by submission.

To be young and passionate shall be accounted shame and punishment.

I will make havoc of Diana's nymphs, my temple shall be dyed with maidens' blood, and there shall be nothing more vile than to be a maiden.

Enter **Diana** *with her* **Nymphs** (*including* **Hebe**). [**Diana** *speaks BSL.*]

Diana
O Neptune, hast thou forgotten thy self, or wilt thou clean forsake me? Hath Diana therefore brought danger to her nymphs, because they be chaste? Shall virtue suffer both pain and shame, which always deserveth praise and honour?

Enter **Venus**. [**Venus** *speaks BSL.*]

Venus (*she ass-kisses* **Neptune**)
Show thyself the same Neptune that I knew thee to be when thou wast younger, and let not Venus' words be vain in thine ears, since thine were imprinted in my heart.

It seems to be commendable to be coy, and honourable to be peevish.

But this is she that hateth sweet delights, envieth loving desires, masketh wanton eyes, stoppeth amorous ears, bridleth youthful mouths, and under a name, or a word 'constancy', entertaineth all kind of cruelty.

Diana *throws magic at* **Venus**.

Venus
She hath taken my son Cupid, Cupid my lovely son, using him like a 'prentice, whipping him cruelly, scorning him like a beast.

Therefore, Neptune I entreat thee, if Venus can do anything, let her try it in this one thing, that thou evil entreat this goddess of hate.

Neptune

I muse not a little to see you two in this place, at this time, and about this matter. But what say you, Diana; have you Cupid captive?

Diana

I say there is nothing more vain than to dispute with Venus, whose untamed affections have bred more brawls in heaven than is fit to repeat in earth. I have Cupid, and will keep him. Not to dandle in my lap, whom I abhor in my heart, but to laugh him to scorn

Venus *throws magic at* **Diana**.

Diana

/ That hath made in my maidens' hearts such deep scars!

Venus

Scars?

No. My son is strong. His power will pierce hearts and make them bleed.

You are weak – you think if you get hit by Cupid's arrows you feel nothing? When first you are hit – the wound is inflamed. But when it is removed you will be dead inside.

Diana *throws magic at* **Venus**.

Therefore, Neptune, if ever Venus stood thee in stead, furthered thy fancies, or has at all times been at thy command, let either Diana keep her chastity and bring her maidens to a continual massacre, or . . . release Cupid of his martyrdom.

Diana

It is known, Venus, that your tongue is as unruly as your thoughts, and your thoughts as unstaid as your eyes.

They prepare to fight.

Diana

Diana does not talk idly. Venus is cheap. She has become insignificant.

Venus

It is an honour for Diana to have Venus mean ill, when she so speaketh well. But you shall see I come not to trifle.

They fight, and while **Diana** *has* **Venus** *in a chokehold:*

Venus

If you love me, help me!

Neptune *uses his power to break them apart.*

Neptune

It were unfit that goddesses should strive, and it were unreasonable that I should not yield. And therefore to please both, both attend!

Diana I must honour; her virtue deserveth no less. But Venus I must love, I must confess so much.

Diana, if you restore Cupid to Venus, I will forever release the sacrifice of maidens. Answer what you will do.

Diana

I account not the choice hard. I yield.

Venus *is relieved.*

Diana

Had I twenty Cupids, I would deliver them all to save one maiden, knowing love to be a thing of all the vainest, chastity to be a virtue of all the noblest. And now shall it be said that Cupid saved those he thought to spoil.

Venus

I agree to this willingly: for I will be wary how my child wanders again. But Diana cannot forbid him to wound.

Diana

Yes, chastity is not within the level of his bow.

Venus

But beauty is an acceptable mark to hit.

Diana *and* **Venus** *knock heads together.* **Neptune** *separates them.*

Neptune

Well, I am glad you are agreed: and say that Neptune hath dealt well with Beauty and Chastity.

Cupid *is brought forward.* [**Cupid** *speaks BSL or ENG.*]

Diana

Here, take your child.

Venus

Sir boy, where have you been? Always taken, first by Sappho, now by Diana. How happeneth it, you unhappy elf?

Cupid

Coming through Diana's woods, and seeing so many fresh faces with fond hearts, I thought for my sport to make them smart, and so was taken by Diana.

Venus

I am glad I have you.

Diana

And I am glad I am rid of them.

Venus (*looking at* **Cupid** *for the first time properly*)

Alas, my poor child, thy wings clipped? Thy brands quenched? Thy bow burnt? And thy arrows broke?

Cupid

Aye, but it skilleth not. I bear now mine arrows in mine eyes, my wings on my thoughts, my brands in mine ears, my bow in my mouth, so as I can wound with looking, fly with thinking, burn with hearing, shoot with speaking.

Venus
Well, you shall up to heaven with me, for on earth thou wilt lose me.

Enter **Tityrus** *and* **Melebeus**. [*They speak ENG –* **Melebeus** *may speak BSL as appropriate.*]

Neptune
But soft, what be these?

Tityrus
Those that have offended thee to save their daughters.

Neptune
Why, had you a daughter?

Tityrus
Aye, and Melebeus a daughter.

Neptune
Where be they?

Melebeus
In yonder woods, and methinks I see them coming.

Enter **Galatea**, **Phillida**, **Peter** *and* **Rafe**. [*They speak ENG.*]

Neptune
Well, your deserts have not gotten pardon, but these goddesses' jars.

Melebeus
This is my daughter, my sweet Phillida.

Tityrus
And this is my beautiful Galatea.

Galatea (*feigning surprise*)
Unfortunate Galatea, if this be Phillida.

Phillida (*likewise*)
Accursed Phillida if that be Galatea.

Galatea

And was I all this while enamoured of Phillida, that sweet Phillida?

Phillida

And could I dote upon the face of a maiden, myself being one, on the face of fine Galatea?

Neptune

Do you both being maidens love one another?

Phillida

I had thought the habit agreeable with the person, and so burned in the fire of mine own fancies.

Galatea

I had thought that in the attire of a boy, there could not have lodged the body of a maiden, and so was inflamed with a sweet desire.

Diana

Now things falling out as they do, you must leave these fond, fond affections. Nature will have it so, necessity must.

A breath – is it really over for the lovers? But then . . .

Galatea

I will never love any but Phillida; her love is engraven in my heart, with her eyes.

Phillida

Nor I any but Galatea, whose faith is imprinted in my thoughts by their words.

Neptune

An idle choice, strange, and foolish, for one maiden to dote on another, and to imagine a constant faith, where there can be no cause of affection. How like you this, Venus?

Venus

I like well and allow it. They shall both be possessed of their wishes, for never shall it be said that Nature or

Fortune shall overthrow Love and Faith.
Is your love unspotted, begun with truth, continued with
constancy, and not to be altered 'til death?

Galatea
Die, Galatea, if thy love be not so.

Phillida
Accursed be thou, Phillida, if thy love be not so.

Diana
Suppose all this, Venus, what then?

Venus
What then? Then these lovers shall love.
Let them take off their disguises, for their love to be true.

Phillida *excited to dress fully as herself again,* **Galatea** *hesitates.*

Venus
Or then shall it be seen, that I can turn one of them to be a
man, and that I will.

Diana
Is it possible?

Venus
What is to love, or the mistress of love, unpossible? How
say ye, are ye agreed, one to be a boy presently?

Tityrus
I am content, because she is a goddess.

Venus
Neptune, you will not dislike it?

Neptune
Not I.

Venus
Nor you Diana.

Diana
Not I.

Venus
Cupid shall not.

Cupid
I will not.

Venus *gets ready to do the gender-change spell.*

Peter
Woah, woah, it doesn't work like that! Don't they get a
choice? You can't just come and wave your magic wand.
You just want to make it neat and cute and tie everything
up with a little bow, but that's not it, babes. People always
think it's just as simple as . . .

He remembers he's talking to a goddess.

. . . I just mean that it's not always as simple as girl to boy,
one thing to another thing, binary to binary, this way or
that. We're humans, we're messy, we're complicated, we're
multifaceted and that's beautiful, that's fierce, that's where
the magic lies.

These two aren't the ones that need fixing, it's

He gestures broadly at everything.

. . . you know?

Phillida
It's the sideways looks, it's the razor-tipped questions, it's
the five-year waiting lists, it's the hatred in the papers. It's
being the punchline to the jokes, it's the violence.

Rafe
It's explaining yourself over and over to people who are
determined to misunderstand you, or it's existing in
fearful secrecy. It's rejection from those who should love
you, it's being framed as a threat or a problem or an
inconvenience.

Phillida
It's trying to keep yourself safe by second guessing what

people might think of you and how they might react so that even if you do get through the day without being shamed, mistreated or attacked, it's already happened inside your head anyway. (*To* **Galatea**.) We haven't even asked you what you want.

Galatea

I want . . . I don't know. I want to not have to know. I want to not always know and be loved anyway! I want . . . to just be. I want to be and to love, and I don't need to be understood. And I appreciate the offer but I think I am exactly who I want to be today. Tomorrow that might change.

Peter

Right?! The magic isn't in the changing, there is no one singular brilliant moment of transformation that fixes everything. The magic is in us, it's that we choose, that we open ourselves to uncertainty and change and learn ourselves through it, the trans magic is what can't be pinned down.

Venus

It seems, even the Goddess of Love can learn. (*She asks* **Galatea**.) Doth it suffice?

Galatea

And satisfy us both, doth it not, Phillida?

Phillida

Yes, Galatea.

Venus

Then let us depart. And we shall bring these lovers together in celebration. One they shall be.

Diana (*referring to* **Peter** *and* **Rafe**)

Who are these that so malapertly thrust themselves into our companies?

Peter

Forsooth, madam, we are fortune tellers.

Venus

Fortune-tellers, tell me my fortune.

Rafe

We do not mean fortune-tellers, we mean fortune tellers:

Peter

We can tell what fortune we have had in the woods.

Rafe   We can tell our story.

Venus [*signs ASL*]

Then shall ye go with us, and share your story, before the party. And we will listen with love. Are you content?

Rafe

Content? Never better content.

Venus

Then follow us!

There is a song! It feels like a party.

Epilogue

Galatea

Go all, 'tis I only that conclude all.

When you leave this place, take with you all that you have seen. You have seen that trans love is vital, that queerness pleases the gods, that when we are permitted to love outside of the script, to love despite the narratives we were taught, to love outside of ownership and tradition, this is when we might find the truest of freedom.

Yield to love, which lurks under your eyelids whilst you sleep, and plays with your heart strings whilst you wake, whose sweetness never breeds sickliness, nor labour weariness, nor grief bitterness. Rise up against those who would try to forbid this love.

When those in our society who are named extremists are merely those fighting for our autonomy of our own desires, definitions, and destinies, then we have a society that is scared of all the brilliances that people can be. Then we have a curse that has settled for too long, an intervention that is bubbling at the borders, a society we must fight to fix.

Ever creeping is the control over where, when, and how we are allowed to speak out, see how Diana's nymphs never stopped pushing back at Neptune's tyranny, never fell silent when their voices were needed. Might we find diverse methods of protest, and never find ourselves without means, be it on the street or on the stage, in crowds or behind doors, in the intensity of our rage, or the ferocity of our loving, in the voices we hold space for, in the narratives we resist and unpick and reshape.

Let Venus fan the flames of our defiance, defying those who restrict the free movement, exploit the labour, or warp the narratives of those with quieter voices, carrying heavier loads, behind fences, gates and borders.

Let it be born from love, this love that is impossible to resist; that is infallible; that is ever changing; that inspires change.

So, change.

Finis.